Fallen Pieces of the Moon

Fallen Pieces of the Moon

Robin Lloyd-Jones

Whittles Publishing

Published by
Whittles Publishing,
Dunbeath Mains Cottages,
Dunbeath,
Caithness KW6 6EY,
Scotland, UK
www.whittlespublishing.com

ISBN 978-1904445-31-9

Contents

Acknowledgements

I would like to express my gratitude to the Scottish Arts Council for its support in writing this book, and to Archie Sinclair for his helpful comments on the early drafts. Thanks are due to my paddling companions in the Nuuk Fjords for their good fellowship, and to those at Black Feather who made the experience possible.

The enthusiasm of Keith Whittles and Elaine Rowan of Whittles Publishing has guided my adventure into print, for which I am grateful.

Thanks must be extended to Chuck Copeland, Heather Boswell and Marc Lebeau, paddling companions, and Ken Nicol, who visited Greenland in 2005 on a separate trip, for permission to use their photographs.

And finally, I would like to say a grateful thank you to my wife, Sallie, not only for drawing the illustrations, but also for understanding my need for places like Greenland.

Introduction

This book is about a kayak trip along the west coast of Greenland, paddling about 150 miles of coastline in the Nuuk fjords area. Icebergs like fallen pieces of the moon, turreted fairy-tale peaks, glistening snowfields, waterfalls plunging over immense cliffs into the sea, a million tons of ice capsizing – these things are the context in which we catch glimpses of Inuit culture and of Arctic animals, and begin to understand the hardships endured by the Viking settlers and explorers like Frobisher and Franklin. This is not so much an expedition book, filled with lists of food and equipment, as a celebration of a sparse, billion-year-old landscape where the roots of things, both physical and human, seem less hidden.

The explorer, Elisha Kent Kane, recorded the words of a companion overawed by the beauty of West Greenland: 'Maybe we have lived only to be here now.' If this book communicates something of the wonder and awe that Greenland inspires, and persuades even one person that its environment is worth preserving, I shall be well pleased.

Figure Captions

Figure Captions (continued)

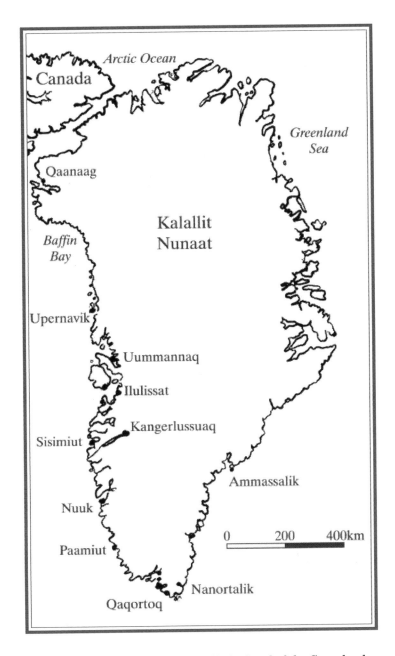

Map of Kalaallit Nunaat, Greenlandic for Land of the Greenlanders

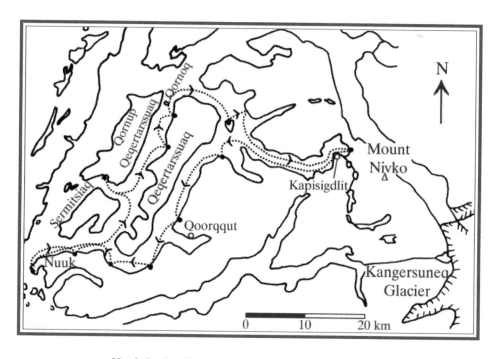

Nuuk fjords, the setting for our 13-day, 120-mile long trip

● *Overnight stops*　　●●● *Canoe route*

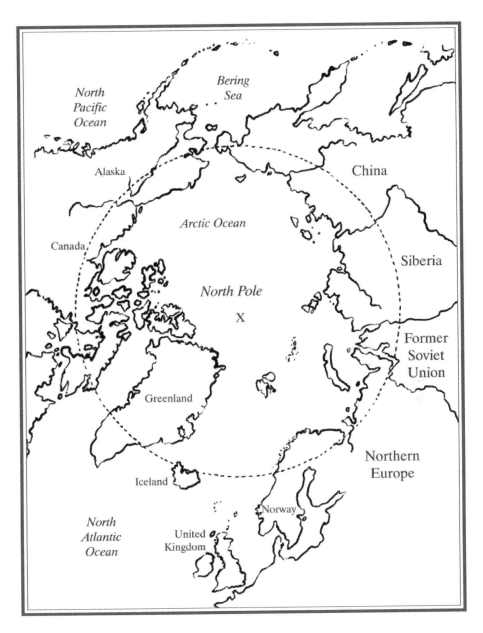

Circumpolar diagram, highlighting the close proximity of the Arctic countries

Of Bergy Bits and Bears

The waiting room at Ottawa airport was like a gateway to another world. Thickset people with dark, straight hair and copper skins conversed in Chipewayan, Cree, Dogrib and Inuktitut. And on the flight boards were names like Coppermine, Igloolik, Resolution Bay, Kuujjuaq. The call came to board the plane to Iqaluit on Baffin Island, my stepping-stone to Kalaallit Nunaat: Greenland. Our objective was to kayak round the Nuuk fjords on Greenland's west coast during the month of July, ending up where we had begun. Thirteen days to cover approximately 120 miles was a fairly leisurely schedule, I thought — before I started.

It had taken me more than a year of planning to reach this moment. My starting point was the Expedition Advisory Centre, a section of the Royal Geographical Society in London. There, amongst maps of uninhabited terrain, on which a printed name was as intrusive as a spider in a bath, I spent happy hours. There too are the reports of most of the expeditions of any note that leave Britain for far-flung corners of the world. I read the reports of all the expeditions which had been to Greenland in the last five years, some for scientific purposes, some to scale unclimbed peaks, some to kayak in Arctic waters where few modern paddlers had been before. The Expedition Advisory Centre also provides information, advice and training to expeditions undertaking research at undergraduate level. However, the sort of thing I had in mind wasn't quite as serious as this. Nor, for that matter, at the age of 58, was I an undergraduate.

Having noted down names and addresses, I followed up several with long phone conversations. A sobering picture of the difficulties and hazards began to emerge. Trying to make me understand how much colder it was in Greenland, one person said, 'The tree line in Greenland stops in Scotland!' I learned about the dangers of various kinds of floating ice. I learned about icebergs, bergy bits and growlers; and about different kinds of ice like frazil, grease ice, shuga and nilas, each coming with its own health warning. And there was no lack of people who positively delighted in recounting tales of sudden storms, aggressive walruses and killer polar bears. Whenever sea ice was the topic its unpredictable behaviour was always mentioned, from one year to the next, from day to day, even from hour to hour. I read about an expedition member who paddled past a smooth, glassy, bubbly piece of ice, about two or three feet in diameter, which suddenly exploded, spraying him and the sea around with frozen fragments. Descriptions of attempts at navigating through the ice were thick with words like chock-a-block, jumbled, packed, choked, and impregnable. Several people spoke of the dangers of being trapped in the pack ice which can close up very quickly if an onshore wind sets in, and of being unable to leave a bay, perhaps for days or even weeks, until the wind dropped or shifted. The speed with which severe storms blew up and the way the weather continually changed was emphasised again and again. As the saying goes in Greenland, 'If you don't like the weather, wait five minutes'. The overall message that came through was that Arctic conditions should be treated with great caution and respect. Crossing open stretches of water of seven miles or more might be commonplace in Scotland, but in these latitudes, I was warned, they were very serious undertakings.

In planning my trip there were so many things to think about, such as which part of this vast coastline of the biggest island in the world to select for an expedition and how to get there. My initial plan was to go somewhere on the wilder, less inhabited east coast. On this side of Greenland, polar bears are both more numerous and more aggressive. The Greenland government decrees, therefore, that all expeditions to the eastern side must carry a firearm capable of killing a polar bear. This led to getting entangled in regulations for taking a rifle out of Britain and more regulations about bringing one into Greenland. And that was only the beginning, although I learned later that the easiest thing to do was to buy one over there on arrival and sell it back before leaving. The merits of various makes of satellite location beacons had to be considered, and a host of other hurdles to jump too: how to obtain an expedition permit from the Danish Polar Centre; sufficient insurance to pay for a search and rescue (minimum £90,000); special Arctic clothing to be bought, finance to be raised, and, one of the biggest problems, the cost of shipping kayaks and crates of supplies and equipment out there. Denmark still had a virtual monopoly of freight to Greenland (Denmark officially claimed all of Greenland as a colony in the 1660s). All my stuff, it seemed, would have to go via Copenhagen. Another problem was finding people to go with. My usual paddling companions stubbornly insisted on having jobs that failed to include unlimited time off in their conditions of employment. When I argued that work seriously interfered with important things like kayaking and climbing, they mumbled about mortgages. Although I confess I do occasionally paddle solo in Scottish waters, I certainly wasn't about to go off on my own in Greenland — not after all the warnings I'd received.

Then there were all those lists to make: lists of medical supplies, lists of clothing, lists of food and calculations about fuel consumption per day. The old style Arctic and Antarctic expeditions always had pemmican high on their lists. I wasn't even sure what it was. It is, I discovered, a mixture of lean desiccated beef (or buffalo meat) and suet fat, all pressed into a form of cake. I almost began to believe in Mark Twain's spoof account of an ascent of the Riffelberg with its cavalcade of 15 barkeepers, four pastry cooks, three chaplains, one Latinist, a barber, 107 mules and a herd of cows.

In the end, all my problems were solved at one stroke by reading an advertisement in the Seattle-based magazine *Sea Kayaker*. A Canadian wilderness organisation regularly ran expeditions to Greenland. They kept kayaks, tents and all other necessary equipment permanently out there. What is more, all the paperwork and red tape and complicated planning would be done for me. All I had to do was pay my share and get myself to the starting point at Ottawa. Not only did it work out cheaper for me to do it this way, but also there, ready and waiting, would be 12 companions. Nonetheless, I thought hard about whether this was what I wanted. It wouldn't be my expedition, and some of the fun and the fascination of a trip like this lies in getting it all together oneself and gradually seeing it come to fruition, however tedious and frustrating that might be at times. Somehow it seemed a little unadventurous to let someone else take all the responsibility. What was holding me back, I concluded, was some vain desire to see myself, and maybe for others to see me, as an intrepid, macho explorer. The things I really cared about would not be affected if I decided to join the group. The Arctic wilderness would be no less beautiful, the Inuit culture no less interesting. The conditions would be just as challenging. The weather, the harsh environment and the ice didn't care by what arrangements I found myself there. Besides, paddling with 12 unknown companions presented challenges of its own: new personalities to explore, a new group dynamic to be forged. I was comfortable with my regular kayaking buddies, but there is always something new to learn when you meet and paddle with different people. The deciding factor was the realisation that, in my particular circumstances, this was likely to be the only way I would fulfil a long-held dream to kayak in Greenland waters.

The *dramatis personae* for this little adventure were: Chuck and Jane, he a timber merchant in Toronto, she a company secretary; Marc and Guylaine, French Canadians from Ottawa, both doctors; Tom and Carol, the American couple from Atlanta, he a professor of Medieval History, she a university librarian; then there was Louis, another French Canadian from Ottawa, an archivist for the Canadian Parliament; Anne, a teacher in a town near Toronto; and Heather from Ottawa who hadn't made up her mind what to do after getting a degree in History. The three who were already in Nuuk, getting things ready, were the two leaders of the trip: Cathy, a PE teacher in Toronto, formerly an ice hockey international, and Joan, a writer on outdoor and environmental topics who had recently done a 2,000 mile canoe journey from the mouth of the St Lawrence to the Arctic Ocean. Both Cathy and Joan had been to Greenland before. Completing the dozen, and already out there, was Valdemar, a Greenlander, whose home was in Nuuk. Heather grinned at me: 'Since you were the last to join up, that makes you the thirteenth member. If anything goes wrong, we'll know who's to blame.'

Before takeoff we'd already been through the 'done much kayaking, have you?' bit. My late mother-in-law used to refer to being 'out bunned'. I've managed to avoid this traumatic experience, but from my squash-playing days, I know all about being out-humbled. It goes something like this:

'Exactly how good are you?' he enquires as we enter the court, rackets in hand.

'Reasonably good,' I reply. 'I play occasionally for the second team.'

'Well, I'll do my best to give you a game,' comes the modest response, and then he proceeds to demolish me, to reduce me to a panting, quivering pool of sweat, before mentioning, oh so diffidently, that he used to play for England. Thrashed nine-nil at squash, out-humbled ninety-nil.

So when everyone claimed to possess just a nodding acquaintance with the skills of kayaking, I was cautious...for about five minutes. Then it kind of slipped out that, actually, I was a qualified instructor with more than 25 years experience. I did at least keep some of my powder dry by not mentioning the book about sea kayaking I'd had published.

The people on the airplane divided roughly into two camps — those concerned with Arctic realities, the mining, the oil, its strategic importance, the struggle for autonomy and for political and economic power; and those like myself and my companions who mainly saw the Arctic as a last frontier, a chance to capture what we had destroyed for ever in the temperate regions, a place still in touch with its myths. Behind me were a mining engineer, a meteorologist returning to his research station in the north of Baffin Island and a man who had formerly been a geologist. The latter had come to the Arctic to do a three-month survey — that was six years ago. He was now a social worker amongst the Inuit of the area. Across the aisle was an anthropologist on her way to spend time in an Inuit hunting and fishing camp, where for a couple of months during the summer, the settled Inuit returned to a more traditional way of life. She told me with a laugh that this vanishing way of life is studied so avidly that a typical camp family consists of a man, a wife, three children and an anthropologist! She'd heard of a camp in Alaska that had been visited by 45 thesis-seeking anthropologists within one year.

In front of me a group of children were returning from an exchange scheme with a school in Toronto. They seemed subdued. I spoke to them briefly. They didn't really want to go home after experiencing the luxuries of their hosts' homes, the amazing variety of food, the movies, the range of goods in the shopping malls. One girl talked about seeing a horse for the first time in her life; and they all chattered excitedly about their first sight of a real tree, for except for one small valley, Greenland is treeless.

The plane was circling Iqaluit. Until recently it was called Frobisher Bay, named after the Elizabethan explorer, Martin Frobisher, who was commissioned by the Muscovy Company to search for a North West passage to China. In the first instance, though, it was named Frobisher Strait, because that was what Martin Frobisher thought it was. He thought it was the channel leading to Cathay and the west, to a monopoly of trade for the Muscovy Company in spices and silks, and untold wealth. Others were to mistake the mouth of the St Lawrence River, the opening to Hudson Bay and various dead end channels as the much sought North West Passage. That so many commercial companies risked their money and captains risked their ships and the lives of their men in search of the Passage is largely due to a huge underestimate of the circumference of the globe. Any opening from Davis Strait to Hudson Bay was thought of as possibly leading, within a matter of two days or so, to the North Pacific. Navigators of the 16th and 17th centuries had no notion that some 2,000 miles of Arctic sea lay between them and the Pacific, and a further 2,000 before Japan could be reached. Had they known the true distances, many of these attempts would probably never have been made.

Below us were landmarks bearing the names of the Muscovy Company's officials and financial backers: Queen Elizabeth Foreland, Lok Island (Michael Lok, treasurer of the company), Countess of Warwick Sound. What clearly emerges from the first hand accounts of Frobisher's three voyages to Baffin Island (it had no name at that time, except Meta Incognita) is that the Eskimos had been trading with British fishermen and whalers for years before Frobisher's arrival. Whalers did much of the original exploration of North American Arctic waters. These discoveries were seldom publicised because a whaling captain who found new fishing ground preferred to keep the information to himself. Some of the more daring skippers had worked their way well into Baffin Bay decades before John Ross officially discovered it in 1818. Expeditions invariably consulted the whalers before setting out, obtaining semi-secret information without which some of the more famous voyages of discovery would probably have failed. And from the ranks of the whalers came the ice pilots or ice masters who steered the expedition ships through the pack ice and the icebergs. No place names testify to the earlier presence of these whalers. Throughout the history of exploration it seems that only Admiralty or officially sponsored expeditions got names onto maps. Needless to say, it didn't occur to anyone that many of these places already had names, the ones given to them by the natives who for centuries had inhabited these 'new' lands.

By chance a stone, picked up by one of Frobisher's sailors as a souvenir, was seen by Michael Lok to glitter. Lok showed it to three different assay masters who all agreed that it was marquise and of little value. So Lok took it to an Italian assayer in London who declared it to be gold, for as he confided to someone later, 'It is necessary to know how to flatter nature and the obsessive desires of your master'.

It was enough to warrant two more expeditions to the area, where the ships were loaded with worthless fool's gold.

Frobisher's voyages to Baffin Island were only one short phase in his career. Joining Francis Drake and John Hawkins, he became a scourge of the Spaniards, participating in every major naval action against them, including the defeat of the Armada. And as for his cargo of stones, brought from Frobisher Strait at such expense and danger, some of it was used to repair roads. The rest was tipped into Bristol harbour.

Just before our plane landed in Iqaluit Tom mentioned a book he had written, *A History of the Ostrogoths*. That was too much. I mean, there's a limit to this humble stuff. I blurted out about my book on kayaking. At least I'd held out until...well, I suppose the trip hadn't really begun.

A large, yellow, plastic box on the runway turned out to be the airport building. The whole town consisted almost entirely of plastic pods, shipped or flown in and put together like a giant Lego set assembled blindfold in a junkyard. Below the word 'IQALUIT' on the side of the building was another word that looked like a cross between Russian script and ancient cuneiform. I hadn't known until that moment that Inuktitut, the language of the Inuit, had its own form of writing.

A magazine in the airport lounge carried advertisements, in Inuktitut and English, saying things like 'Inuktitut is our window to knowing more about who we are, the key to our identity. Be proud of your heritage and learn to speak and write Inuktitut.' I was glad to see they were fighting to keep their language. The world's repository of languages is being eroded even faster than its endangered animals. Half the planet's surviving languages are no longer being learnt by the children of native speakers, which means they are probably beyond the stage of being saved.

Despite the exhortation in the magazine advertisement, Inuktitut, along with many other minority Native American languages, is a second-class language in Canada. English is the language of empowerment. It is the language used by the bosses at all levels, the language of higher education and of the Internet, the language of advancement in the modern world. In Greenland, however, Greenlandic (or *Kalaallisut* to give it its native name; essentially the same as Inuktitut, with a few variations) is the official language, with Danish as the second language. I hope Greenlandic can resist the pressures of the modern world. In a planet where globalisation and standardisation are creeping over us, languages are a celebration of diversity, an expression of relationships peculiar to particular social groups. Languages give us a priceless link with history and allow us a window onto a unique outlook on the world, a whole way of thinking and of mentally constructing the world that is not our way. One very small illustration of this is that Inuktitut, along with most other Canadian Arctic languages, ranks 'you' forms of speech over 'I' forms of speech. Speakers of these languages would not place themselves at the centre by saying, 'I see you'. Instead they would say, 'You are seen by me'.

With the help of the Language Centre at Glasgow University, I had dipped a toe into the deep mysteries of Inuktitut. One beginners' manual, the size of a telephone directory, cheerfully stated 'When you finish this you will not have reached the end of the beginning'.

Inuktitut is a polysynthetic language in which ideas are strung together like beads on a string. In Greenland (where the western alphabet is sometimes used) a newspaper headline announcing a harpoon throwing competition read: 'Unammmineq naakkiarneqqortusaanneq toraajunequssaanneq.'

Everyone knows that Inuktitut has more than 30 different words for snow and as many for ice. This is hardly surprising considering that snow and ice conditions can be a matter of life or death, of a successful catch or starvation, of fast travel or weary hours with almost no progress. What is not so well known is that there is no one general word for snow, such a vague, unspecific description being of little help to Inuit survival. In a similar vein, although I know only the word potato, a potato farmer will have words for more than 50 varieties. I've been told that Gaelic has 17 words for rain. Incidentally, Gaelic speakers assure me (with a quiet smile) that no word exists in their language to convey quite the same degree of urgency as the word *mañana*.

Chuck, Jane and I took a short walk through Iqaluit, a depressing experience. So many faces were closed, inward looking, blank. People staggered drunkenly, even this early in the afternoon or looked right through me with drug-glazed eyes, people who lived on welfare cheques and government handouts, people who had lost contact with their old hunting culture, but not found a place in western culture. The suicide rate, I learned, was very high. There is a new term for indigenous people such as these Baffin Islanders who are locked into nations they can never hope to rule — they are said to belong to a Fourth World.

They hadn't surrendered to their fate, though. The headlines in the local newspaper, *Nunatsiaq News*, were about how hundreds of Iqaluit residents, Inuit and non-Inuit, had marched in protest against a lifestyle that was harming their children.

As we wandered through the mud, I told Chuck and Jane about a passage I'd come across in the *Lonely Planet* guide which said that in 1941 the United States military moved into Greenland and set up a base at Narsarsuaq (also known as Blue West One or Bluie West). It was here that, throughout World War Two and the Korean War, the Americans sent their hopeless casualties: those so badly injured in battle they would have dampened the war enthusiasm of the American public had they gone home. No patient sent to Narsarsuaq ever left; families of these victims were sent a bottle of ashes and told their soldier had been killed in action. It was just one paragraph, tucked away amongst a host of other information, but it has haunted me ever since I read it.

Inside the spacious, igloo-like dome that was St Jude's Anglican Cathedral, two dog sleds, turned on their sides, their wooden runners polished, formed the altar railings. Above the altar was a cross of narwhal tusks. The narwhal (or *tugalik*) is the small whale of the High Arctic, which has a single tusk spiralling out of its head. Its only close relative is the beluga, or Arctic white whale.

On the way back to the airport I looked in the window of a shop selling carvings for tourists. Carving has always been an essential Inuit skill. From bone, stone, walrus ivory, whale teeth or caribou or musk ox horn, they fashioned toggles for dog harnesses, spoons, cooking pots, harpoons, fish spears or sled parts. They also made carvings of the animals they hunted to please their spirits so that these creatures would offer themselves to be killed. And the Inuit carved designs on their harpoons lest an ill-made weapon, lacking decoration, might insult the seals and cause them to leave the area. A chess set in the window caught my eye. The rooks were igloos, the bishops dogs, the knights polar bears. The King and Queen were Inuit in full regalia and the pawns were fat little Arctic owls.

Air travel in the Arctic has been described as an ever-decreasing size of plane and an ever-increasing dependence on the weather. And, sure enough, the plane squatting on the runway, backed by a grey, ice-flecked sea was noticeably smaller. After the obligatory jokes about winding up the rubber band and handing out the parachutes, we took bets, not whether it would leave on time, but how long it would be delayed. The word *imaaqa* (maybe) is the most frequently used word in the Inuktitut language. It's the unpredictable behaviour of pack ice and icebergs and the uncertainty of the weather that does it, the sudden violent winds which appear out of nowhere and blow for days, dense fogs which brew up within minutes from a clear blue sky. Delays are so common that, until recently, the local airlines didn't refund the cost of hotel bills while you waited for the weather to clear: and you could find yourself waiting anything up to a week. I read of one American kayaker in Baffin Island who, on asking what sort of weather to expect later in the day, said people gave him the kind of look he'd get from New Yorkers if he'd asked for next year's stock market forecast. Thinking about this reminded me of a slide lecture I attended given by John Dunn, a Scottish Arctic traveller, who made a 3,000 kilometre traverse of Baffin Island by ski, kayak and on foot, taking 192 days. One of the things that stuck in my mind was his account of how, not wanting to pollute the wilderness, he made a huge parcel of his garbage and, at the first trading post he came to, posted it back home to his wife. Unfortunately, he'd forgotten to tell her he was going to do this and she opened it expecting some exotic and wonderful present. 'Will passengers for Nuuk board now,' crackled the intercom. Amazingly, we were departing on time.

We rose above Iqaluit, flying north along the coast, preparing to head across Davis Strait. John Davis entered this ice-ridden stretch between Baffin Island and Greenland in 1584 (six years after Frobisher's third and last voyage to this area). Despite the cramped conditions in his small ships, Davis took an orchestra along with him. Off the coast of Greenland, when Eskimos approached cautiously in their kayaks to see who these strangers were, Davis called upon his orchestra to play and directed his officers and men to dance. This was typical of his dealings with them. His courteous regard for the Eskimos is unique in early arctic narratives. Small wonder he found the Eskimos to be a 'very tractable people, void of craft or double dealing, and easy to be brought to any civility or good order.' Then in 1616, the year Shakespeare died, William Baffin sailed up Davis Strait and reached a northerly latitude that remained unequalled in those waters for over two centuries.

Below us was Countess of Warwick Sound. It was here, in 1861, that the American explorer Charles Francis Hall found piles of coal. Eskimo oral tradition identified it as having been unloaded from Martin Frobisher's ships 300 years earlier. Hall was on Baffin Island on one of his several quests to find Sir John Franklin and his men who had never returned from their bid to find the still elusive North West passage. On another July day, in 1845, the two ships *Erebus* and *Terror*, with 130 officers and men under the command of Sir John Franklin, set sail from the west coast of Greenland. It was the most technologically advanced expedition ever seen, the Apollo programme of its day. The ships were iron plated, powered by locomotive engines as well as by sail, and steam heated. On board they carried the world's first cameras, desalinators and a recent innovation – canned food. In late July, whalers in Baffin Bay spotted Franklin's two ships. They were never seen again, by white men that is. Over the next two decades, more than 50 expeditions scoured the Arctic in search of Franklin and his men, at first searching for survivors, and then for bodies or any clue that might help solve the mystery. When Hall first took up the search, they had been missing for over ten years. He entertained hopes, however, that a handful of them might still be alive, sustained by some remote Eskimo community. Hall scattered the names of friends and patrons around the arctic landscape with largesse. There is a Cornelius Grinnell Bay (after the son of Henry Grinnell, his main backer), a Pugh Island (US Senator), a Hamlin's Bay (his dentist), and even one bleak stretch of water bearing the name of Cincinnati Press Channel. The river at the head of Frobisher Bay, Hall named Cynthia Grinnell River. Unfortunately, on returning home, he found that his friend's daughter was called Sylvia, not Cynthia.

Sir John Franklin

Crew of HMS Terror *breaking a passage through the ice (George Back, Library and Archives Canada, C-028848)*

Hauling sledges on the Belcher expedition, 1850 (W W May, Library and Archives Canada, C-006699)

Some nine months after looking down on the scene of Hall's explorations, I found myself at the Smithsonian Institution in Washington with Hall's actual journal in my hand. To my surprise, the Hall papers were kept in old shoeboxes and used brown envelopes, unsorted and uncatalogued. Although Hall's Baffin Island papers were there, the journal of his Polaris expedition which attempted to push as far north as possible, are missing, presumed lost on the ice during the process of breaking camp. As a librarian at the Smithsonian said to me, 'So much good historical paper has been lost to the winds and the snow north of latitude 60'. In my first foray into these jumbled sheaves, I encountered a scrap of paper with the cryptic comment: 'reindeer tongue tastes better raw than cooked'. And a letter from a friend, dated May 1864, explaining that the word *esquimaux* came from a Cree Indian word meaning 'eater of raw meat'. Then I came upon the actual journal of his first expedition to Baffin Island, written in brown ink on cheap, ruled paper, in rather illegible handwriting possibly because his fingers were numb with cold. In this journal he recounts how the Eskimos had known all along that what the white men had named Frobisher Strait was, in fact, a bay and not the opening to a North West passage that Frobisher thought it was. In Hall's scribbled hand, I read:

> *I ran my finger along the chart in Frobisher Strait, showing them the track I intended to follow. When I got up to about Longitude 72, they stopped me, crying 'ar-gi! ar-gi!' (No! No!). They then took hold of my hand, moving it around till it connected with Meta Incognita.*

Frobisher was certainly not the only one to make errors of that kind. The story of naval exploration is full of false discoveries. Well into the 20th century atlases showed islands that we now know do not exist. The British Admiralty Pacific Chart of 1875 showed 142 non-existent islands: a mixed bag of poor navigation, misprints, optical illusions, wild tales, wishful thinking and deliberate fraud. Arctic waters were, and still are, particularly prone to false sightings. In fog, large icebergs can easily be mistaken for islands or headlands; frozen sea can be taken for land or vice-versa; and, due to refraction in layers of cold air, all sorts of mirages, *fata morgana* (inverted images) and other optical illusions occur. For instance, Crocker Land, reported by Peary, rising out of the Polar Sea, does not exist, nor does Charles Frances Hall's President's Land; and King Oscar Land, sighted from Frans Joseph Land (north of Spitzbergen) in 1884, has never been seen again. When an area is explored for the first time, what is observed and 'found' is influenced by how that land is already imagined, what you expect to see, what you are looking for and what can be fitted into an existing framework of preconceptions. No doubt, the way I see Greenland is subject to a similar process.

Hall and two Eskimos in Arctic clothing (from Hall's Arctic Researches)

Hall was one of the first Arctic explorers to realise that the Eskimos could not have lived for centuries in such a hostile environment without knowing what they were doing. He wore furs like they did, used dog sledges and adopted many of their ways. Up until this point, particularly amongst the British officers of the Royal Navy, the Eskimos were regarded as ignorant savages. All over Queen Victoria's empire to be seen to be 'going native' was a guarantee of exclusion from polite society. The caricature of the British explorer sitting alone over a meal in the jungle in full evening dress is not so far from the truth. Franklin's expedition, hauling boats across the frozen sea in a desperate bid for survival after the ice had crushed their ships, still carried silver plates and cutlery and dress uniforms with equipment for polishing the brass buttons. Those who voiced the opinion that there might be lessons to be learned from the Eskimos were regarded as unsporting, breaking the rules in the manly game of Arctic exploration and resorting, as Franklin put it, to some kind of 'grubby subterfuge'. Such was the attitude of the Victorian ruling classes to those beneath them that the crew of many an expedition ship felt closer to the Eskimos than they did to their own officers. The lack of understanding of the Inuit culture is illustrated by an incident which took place in the 1830s, when John Ross, exploring in the Boothia Felix region, tried to prevent an Eskimo family from building an igloo too close to his ship, saying that he had claimed the land in the name of the King. To Ross, a house was something permanent, whereas to the Eskimos it was something temporary, easily abandoned in a few hours. And it had not occurred to the Eskimos that anybody owned the land anymore than they owned the sea or the air.

I talked of these things to Heather as we passed over Davis Strait. She quoted to me bits of the famous speech made by Chief Seattle of the Suquamish tribe:

> *This we know. The earth does not belong to man, man belongs to the earth ... How can you buy and sell the sky, the warmth of the land? The idea is strange to us ... the rivers are our brothers ... the air is precious ... for all things share the same breath.*

Almost a year later, I discovered that Chief Seattle never spoke these words. It is an interesting example of how a myth can start and grow. In 1854 he did make a speech in what is now downtown Seattle to Governor Stevens, a man who firmly believed that the only good Indian was a dead Indian. The first version of the speech in English was published 30 years after it was made and its style has every appearance of false memory syndrome and of reflecting the literary aspirations of the recorder and translator, Dr Henry Smith, more than the actual words of the orator. Subsequent versions, written by environmentalists, have tended to include what the chief should have said, or what the authors would have liked him to say. Some versions even mention trains, which Chief Seattle had never seen and knew nothing about, and the slaughter of buffalo on the Great Plains, which began years after his death. The most famous version, the one quoted in good faith by Heather, was written by a screenwriter, Ted Perry, for the 1972 film about pollution and ecology, *Home*. The film's producers revised Perry's script without his knowledge, removed his name from the credits and sent off 18,000 posters with the speech on it to viewers who requested it.

The legend of Chief Seattle's great speech may never die. I feel that the story of Franklin's last expedition, like the story of the *Titanic* or of Ghandi is, in some ways, similar. Every generation has its own interpretation of these stories, its own version that reflects its preoccupations, struggles and deep-seated needs. Like the story of Scott's dash to the South Pole, Franklin's last expedition has, at different times, been seen as an example of true British grit and bravery, as a tale of disaster brought on by arrogance and entrenched attitudes, and as a microcosm of a snobbish and class-ridden society. Perhaps, in years to come, as our planet heads towards ecological disaster, we will see them as the first polluters of the last unspoiled places on Earth, as the people who opened up the way for worse to come. My own view is that we cannot judge people outside the context of their times. They believed that what they did was for the best and they were brave men.

Hall was one of the first westerners to look at Inuit culture in a different way and to learn from it. A more widespread interest in their culture, however, did not really start until the second and third decades of the 20th century. Vilhjalmur Stefansson headed the Canadian Arctic Expedition in 1913 and spent a number of years learning to live with the Inuit. Robert Flaherty spent time in the North as a prospector and explorer. He began filming life in the North to pass the time, but soon became a serious filmmaker and his silent film *Nanook of the North* was, for the general public, their first real insight into Eskimo life. Flaherty was perhaps the first person to truly appreciate the art of the Inuit and his sculpture collection is one of the finest in the world. Then there was the Inuktitut-speaking Knud Rasmussen, organiser of the Danish Fifth Thule Expedition of 1921–24, whose mother was a Greenland Inuit woman. Rasmussen made a study of the Inuit across the whole of Arctic North America. The expedition's report is ten volumes long and contains an impressive collection of Inuit stories, poems, legends and drawings.

'I don't like the look of that!' said Guylaine, pointing out of the cabin window. In every direction Davis Strait was choked with pack ice. How much ice we would encounter in the Nuuk fjords was one of the uncertainties of our trip. It depended on two factors: firstly, the extent to which the pack ice, over which we were now passing, drifted into the fjord system; secondly, from the landward end, the size and number of icebergs which the large glacier at the head of Kangersuneq Fjord was calving this year and pushing down the fjord into our path. We contemplated the pack ice in silence.

'What are you chuckling about?' Guylaine asked.

'I've just remembered something about this guy Hall.'

I told her about the occasion, recorded in his journal, when one of his sailors had to have several frostbitten toes amputated without benefit of any form of anaesthetic. As one of his toes was being cut off, the sailor cried out in pain, 'Damn that toe to hell!' Hall, a religious man, was so shocked by this outburst that he wrote in his journal: 'It was enough to make one's blood run cold so extraordinarily wicked was the speech.'

I thought about the cross made of narwhal tusks in the Anglican cathedral at Iqaluit. The majority of the world's narwhal population is found in the waters over which we were now flying. In mature males the tusk, with its left-hand spiral, may reach a length of more than nine feet and weigh over 52 pounds. Young narwhals of both sexes have two teeth embedded in the upper jaw. The left tooth of the male erupts to form the tusk. Very occasionally, the right tooth also develops to produce a rare double tusker. The exact purpose of these tusks is not known. The most reasonable explanation seems to be that, like antlers, they are a secondary sexual characteristic of males, for display and for establishing dominance rather than for fighting with. The narwhal is still an important source of food to the people in this area. The Canadian government operates a community quota scheme. However, this annual quota applies to the number actually caught and not to the number killed. When the narwhal come into the bays and inlets, the hunters go out in their motorboats and blaze away with their rifles. Many sink and are lost or are severely wounded and escape to die later. The hunters kill at least twice as many as they manage to retrieve. Every hunter receives a share in proportion to his contribution to the hunt. And anyone can come to the beach to claim a portion of the whale simply by touching it. In this way, the old and disabled are fed, too. The main natural enemy of the narwhal is the killer whale, or orca. The orca is the undisputed king of the sea, feared by men and animals alike. They hunt the narwhal in pairs, crushing it between their two bodies. The Greenland whale, they hunt in a different fashion. Again working in pairs, one bites the Greenland whale's lip to force it to open its mouth, while the other thrusts itself into the vast mouth and tears out its tongue. Orcas, however, are frightened of walruses. The Inuit know this and cup their hands and bellow into the water like a walrus.

In the Middle Ages, the narwhals' tusk was believed to be the horn of the fabled unicorn, the beast that was too proud to board Noah's ark, but somehow survived. Strictly speaking, a tusk is essentially a tooth, made of ivory while a horn is made of the same stuff as hair, nails and hooves, but details like this didn't bother our medieval ancestors. To a unicorn's horn were attributed all sorts of magical properties. It was said to cure the plague and the pox, make barren women fertile and impotent men potent. A Swiss physician of the mid 16th century wrote: 'This horn is useful and beneficial against epilepsy. It will cure pestilent fever, rabies, proliferation and infestation of vermin and destroy the worms within the body from which children faint'. From all over Europe the sick made pilgrimage to the monastery of Saint Denis near Paris, where they could drink from the marble basin in which stood a seven-foot long unicorn horn. Powdered unicorn horn was thought to be an antidote to poison. Moreover, a horn could detect the presence of poison in food, making it froth darkly and bubble. In an age when plotting and political assassinations were common and poison was the chosen method of dispatch, it is no wonder that those in power were willing to pay astronomical prices for the magical horn — ten times its weight in gold. Horns, set in gold, stood on many royal dining tables to provide a warning of poison. Those who traded for narwhal tusks with the Inuit must, of course, have known that they were not unicorns' horns. It was one of the best-kept trade secrets the world has ever known.

I had wondered whether I might see a whale as we crossed to Greenland. Davis Strait and Baffin Bay were once one of the busiest whaling grounds in the world. Whale oil was needed to light the oil lamps in the homes and streets of Europe and America, to lubricate machinery and process coarse wool in the textile mills. Whalebone (baleen) was turned into umbrella and parasol ribs, corset stays, hoops for dresses, Venetian blinds, coach and furniture springs, fishing rods and a host of other things where its tough, light, springy qualities could be put to use. After flenching (or flensing) in which the layer of blubber was cut away from the carcass, the 20 tons or more of meat on the carcass (the crang) was left to rot in the water or on bloody ice floes. The early 1820s were the halcyon days of Arctic whaling, with up to 2,000 whales being killed in these waters each year. The main target of the whalers was the Greenland Right whale or bowhead whale. It was called the Right whale because it was the right species to catch, having a higher ratio of blubber to weight than any other whale. A good size fish might yield 25 tons of oil; and its mouth, the size of a large living room, with its plankton-straining curtain of baleen plates, could provide a ton or more of whalebone. The bowhead grows to about 60 feet in length and weighs 100 tons or more. Its tongue alone weighs about one ton. Not surprisingly, the Greenland Right was hunted nearly to extinction. It was not only the marine life that was brought to the brink of extinction by the whalers. Many Inuit communities along the coastline were either wiped out or severely depopulated by diseases brought by the whalers, such as small pox, influenza, even the common cold, against which these isolated settlements had developed no immunity.

Looking down upon the whaling grounds from the comfort of a warm aeroplane, it was difficult to imagine the terrible hardships and dangers endured by the whalers. Every year ships were lost, trapped in the ice and crushed, or sunk in collisions with icebergs in thick fogs. Men drowned, froze to death, were killed in the hazardous moments of grappling with the whales from the small whaleboats, died from starvation or from scurvy or were maimed

Whale fishing, by William Scoresby (courtesy of Whitby Museum)

Whalers in Icefield, by William Scoresby (courtesy of Whitby Museum)

by numerous accidents as well as by frostbite. Scurvy, caused by vitamin C deficiency, produces horrifying effects on the human body. Blood weeps from follicles of the hair, then haemorrhages, causing red blotches all over the body. The legs swell and terrible pain wracks the joints. The gums recede and blacken until teeth loosen and fall out. The body becomes bloated and misshapen; the skin turns yellow and is covered in ulcers. At least death in the open whaleboats was quicker. One blow from the tail of a bowhead whale could smash a boat or kill a man. Their strength was legendary. A bowhead harpooned in these seas once ran out 10,500 yards of thick hemp line, weighing 7,000 pounds, and pulled an entangled 28-foot whaleboat down with it before it was subdued. A harpooned whale might pull its captors for ten miles or more before weakening. This terrifying and exhilarating, high speed tow was dubbed by American whalers 'the Nantucket sleigh ride' (Nantucket and New Bedford being the main east coast whaling ports).

Somewhere over the horizon to the north of us the great whaling fleet disaster of 1830 occurred in Melville Bay. The sea ice started forming much earlier than usual, a constant southerly wind drove the ice up against the shore, concentrating it and forming massive pressure ridges. Nineteen British whaling ships were trapped, crushed and sunk and many more eventually limped home, badly damaged. Accounts of ships over-wintering in the Arctic are full of the terrors of the ice as its grip slowly tightened on a ship, squeezing it as a mailed fist might squeeze an eggshell. Doorframes become twisted so that doors would not shut. Deck planks suddenly sprang upwards. I tried to imagine what it must have been like to lie in a hammock in the darkness of the winter, listening to the cracking and rumbling as immense forces pushed the ice up into new ridges: monstrous claws raking along the outside of the hull; a rivet giving way with a sound like a pistol shot; the tortured ship groaning, quivering and vibrating; the sudden explosion of a beam snapping like a matchstick; the waiting in a state of readiness for the order to abandon ship, and the desolate feeling of leaving what had been your home and place of safety for the last six months or more.

The snow-capped mountains of Greenland ghosted into sight. The sky was overcast, the water gunmetal grey, with the mountains showing themselves in stark black and white. A strong wind was blowing. The plane rocked from side to side as it came in to land. As I stepped onto the runway a freezing wind pierced my inadequate clothing. There was nothing so formal as customs or passport checks or anything of that sort. We simply wandered off the plane into the waiting room and waited for Cathy, Joan and Valdemar. Heather had forewarned me that native Greenlanders don't like being called Eskimos: 'Inuit is better, but Greenlander is better still,' she said. In fact, there has been so much intermarriage that only a minority could now claim to be pure Inuit. One sixth of all Greenlanders now live in Denmark, many forced to go there for economic reasons, and quite a high proportion experiencing difficulties in adjusting to Danish society.

Marc unfolded a map and we gathered round, tracing our proposed route with our fingers. One effect of Greenland's move towards independence (its status now being 'self-governing member of the Kingdom of Denmark') has been a return to Inuktitut place names. Thus, for instance, Godthab is now Nuuk (peninsula) and Jakobshavn is Ilulissat (iceberg). Since maps were not in use among the earlier hunting cultures, the names in effect were the maps and tended to be descriptive. There are, for example, at least half a dozen places called Qeqertarsuaq (big island). The Inuit did not have maps on paper, but early explorers found the Inuit well able to draw accurate maps for them on the ground or in the snow if asked to do so.

The van arrived. We drove towards the seaman's hostel, past brightly coloured, prefabricated wooden houses shipped from Denmark. Nuuk, with a population of about 14,000, is the size of a small market town in Britain and is one of the smallest capitals in the world. Its mainstays are fishing, fish processing, commerce, administration and increasingly, tourism. The Danish influence is very obvious in the housing, the goods and styles in the shops, in

Nuuk, with Sermitsiaaq mountain in the background

people's names. Rearing up above the prefabricated houses, on Store Slette, were several large five-storey housing blocks. The largest of these, Block P, contains about 1% of Greenland's population. These blocks were built to accommodate the small, scattered communities who were centralized on Nuuk by government policy in the 1960s in an attempt to raise health and education standards.

Strolling down a street, replete with coffee and Danish pastries paid for in Danish kroner borrowed from Heather, I came across what claims to be the world's largest post box, part of Father Christmas' Post Office, which receives more than 100,000 letters a year from children all over the world. Peering through the little window in the post box I could see several from Britain. For anyone interested, the official address is: Father Christmas, the North Pole, Father Christmas' Post Office, DK-3900 Nuuk, Greenland.

Beyond the harbour a whale was making its way up the fjord. It was too far away to identify what kind it was. Beluga whales, fin whales, pilot whales and orcas are all found in Greenland waters. Whatever type it was, tomorrow we'd be following it.

Fallen Pieces of the Moon

Next morning, after a night in the seaman's hostel, we walked down to a small bay on the other side of the main harbour. The sky was overcast, but the air smelt clean and fresh. Occasionally the layers of cloud shifted, allowing a glimpse of the snow-capped Sermitsiaaq Mountain across the fjord to the north, its twin peaks and deep hanging valley shaped like a giant saddle. Some of us began carrying the kayaks from the boat shed where they were stored down to an area of barren rock above the waterline, while others unloaded the Land Rover. The piles of supplies, equipment and gear grew and grew until we were convinced it would be absolutely impossible to fit everything into our craft. Rather to my surprise, several of the others had brought small folding chairs with them. This hardly matched my image of the sort of thing needed by macho Arctic paddlers. These items, I failed to notice, belonged to those who had been to the Arctic before.

There were five single fibreglass kayaks and four doubles or tandems as the Canadians called them. On a trip of any length, it is sensible to have at least one double kayak in case someone is taken ill, is injured or becomes exhausted. All the kayaks were equipped with rudders, which could be lowered or lifted, the latter being necessary to avoid damage in shallow water. In Britain, rudders are out of fashion, partly, I think, because the lines and foot pedals by which the rudder is controlled might become entangled with the feet when a hasty exit is called for (although this is far less likely with the latest rudder arrangements); and partly because the type of kayaking done is not so much about paddling long distances on expeditions, but more about sporting amongst skerries, skimming through narrow channels and enjoying the skills of using the paddle to twist and turn and draw sideways.

We spent the morning sorting supplies and equipment and then loading the kayaks. The singles had watertight compartments fore and aft of the cockpit that were accessible through wide hatches on the deck. The canvas doubles didn't have these hatches, making them more difficult to load, it being a long reach up to the extremities of the bow and the stern from the cockpit. Things had to be shoved and prodded into these dark recesses with a paddle. However, like old suitcases, they did have the advantage of being infinitely expandable. Since space is at a premium there is no room for waterproof bags half the bulk of which is simply trapped air, which is why 13 normally harmless people were kneeling and bouncing on bags as if they were all-in wrestlers, or clasping them in fierce bear hugs to expel unwanted air.

Whereas the cockpits of the single kayaks ended in a bulkhead with an adjustable foot rest in front of it, our canvas folding doubles didn't, so that it was a matter of judgment how far towards the cockpit to fill up with gear and how much leg room to leave. Too much could mean hours of cramped, uncomfortable paddling; too little could result in not having anything for the feet to push against, something that is necessary for an efficient paddling stroke because the thrust of the paddle against the water is counterbalanced by the foot on the same side pressing against something. It takes a deal of packing, repacking, punching, kicking and cursing to get it just right. The miracle of making everything disappear into the kayaks never quite happened. Each of us was left with several bags that simply wouldn't fit in. These had to be strapped to the back deck. This is not an ideal solution since it makes the kayak less stable and also raises the craft's low profile so that it catches the wind and makes it harder to steer.

Since we had planned to cover only a short distance on the first day, we had a couple of hours to spare to look around Nuuk before setting out. From Scotland I had made contact with Lars Pieter Danielsen, the president of the Nuuk Kayak Club. Through him I received an invitation to attend the biennial National Kayak Championships at Ilulissat. In the year 2000, the championships were opened up to non-Greenlanders for the first time, not that I'd had any thought of actually taking part. A friend who had tried paddling a genuine Eskimo kayak had advised me, 'Don't even think about it!' Most Inuit are smaller than Europeans and their kayaks are made to measure. I would find it a very tight fit, he said, and would have great difficulty getting out in the event of a capsize and a failure to roll up, which in his

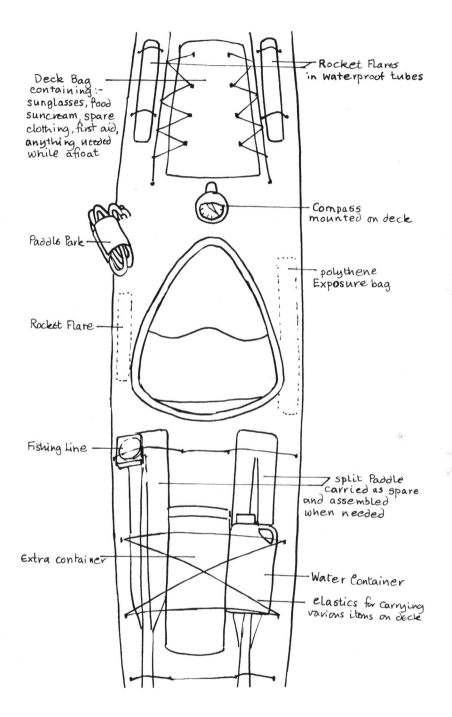

Rocket Flares
in waterproof tubes

Deck Bag
containing :-
sunglasses, food
suncream, spare
clothing, first aid,
anything needed
while afloat

Compass
mounted on deck

Paddle Park

polythene
Exposure bag

Rocket Flare

Fishing Line

split Paddle
Carried as spare
and assembled
when needed

Extra container

Water Container

elastics for carrying
various items on deck

Typical layout on a kayak deck

opinion was quite likely because of the shock of sudden submersion in the extremely cold water completely destroys your orientation and timing unless you are well used to it. So I had to choose between attending the championships as a spectator and doing some active paddling with the Canadian group. It wasn't a difficult choice really.

I had also made contact with John Peterson who won all nine events at the 1989 championships and, in a long distance phone call from Scotland to Greenland, spoke to him before finding myself here in person a couple of months later. His grandfather, he told me, had been a kayak postman, delivering the mail from Nuuk to Maniitsoq, a distance of 112 miles or two days paddle in the open sea. 'Our Inuit culture has left little evidence — no pyramids, palaces or temples,' John said. 'But it has been around for a long time. Perhaps our greatest achievement is to have survived the elements through thousands of Arctic winters.' And, a supreme example of this successful adaptation to an incredibly harsh environment was the kayak (or *qajaq*), a hunting craft superbly suited to the conditions. In the opinion of Nansen the explorer, 'the kayak is far and away the best one-man boat in existence, both as a means of transport and for hunting'. Neither Lars nor John was in Nuuk at the moment, being at the kayak championships in Ilulissat, so I had missed out on the opportunity to meet them. The least I could do, I thought, was to have a look at the Greenland National Museum and Archives in which there was a collection of traditional kayaks, some of them several centuries old.

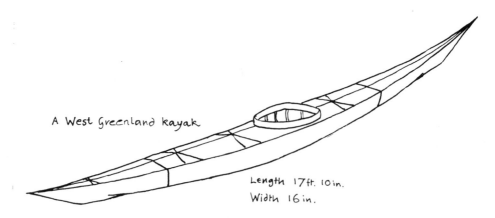

A West Greenland kayak

Length 17ft. 10in.
Width 16in.

A West Greenland kayak

By the middle of the 20th century, the kayak had fallen into disuse in most of Greenland and a whole generation of Greenlanders had virtually no knowledge of it. However, inspired by an exhibit of three ancient kayaks on loan from Holland, some young Greenlanders sought out the few remaining men who still knew how to build and use kayaks and persuaded them to hold training classes. There are now over 2,000 members of the Greenland National Kayak League (or Pequatigiiffiit Qaannat Kalaallit Nuanaanni Kattuffiat), including women (the kayak was traditionally a men's boat). Home Rule has both awakened the Greenlanders' interest in their native culture and whetted their appetite for even greater independence. And both these things find expression in a renaissance of traditional kayaking and in the establishment of national championships.

It would not be accurate, however, to equate pride in their culture with a wish to return to how things were before the white men came. In the days when there were still people alive who remembered those times, they were quite sure that life was now a great deal better than it had been with its almost unimaginable hardships, the terrors of hunger, the cannibalism, the death of so many children, the forced abandonment of aging parents.

> *There is fear*
> *In feeling cold*
> *Come to the great world*
> *And seeing the moon*
> *Follow its old footprints*
> *In the winter night.*　　　　Traditional Inuit Poem

A Greenland trading post in the early 20ᵗʰ Century
(from Arctic Adventure *by Peter Freuchen, 1936)*

The Danish Arctic traveller and writer, Peter Freuchen, who, in the first half the 20th century, came to know the Eskimos better than any white man in the world, records meeting an old woman, Atakutaluk. Starvation had forced her to eat the dead bodies of her husband and her three children. It was a matter for great sorrow, but not for secrecy or shame. Such things were accepted as necessary for survival. Rasmussen records having met an Inuit couple that had 20 children. Of these, ten little girls had been killed by their parents, four had died of disease and one had been killed in a kayak accident. Rasmussen asked the parents if they had regretted killing ten of their baby daughters. The mother said no, because if she'd had to suckle all the girls who were born before the boys she would have no sons now. Despite the hardships and grim realities of Inuit life, explorers and travellers were invariably impressed by the Inuit's cheerfulness, sense of humour and zest for life.

The woman who ate her husband and three children
(from Arctic Adventure *by Peter Freuchen, 1936)*

Cannibalism, of course, has been the last resort of many starving Westerners too: sailors adrift in open boats, gold rush stampeders trapped by winter in some isolated shack, Arctic explorers, and more recently, the Uruguayan rugby team whose aeroplane crashed in the Andes in 1972. In making the decision as to whether or not to eat the flesh of a comrade, the way a starved body copes with the crisis is relevant. The body gradually shuts down all inessential functions until only the heart, the lungs and the brain are kept running. Then the parts of the brain that deal with higher thinking begin to fail, those parts that are responsible for many of our inhibitions. It is usually at this stage that acts of cannibalism occur.

On the way to the museum, I passed The Board, the local fish and game market, which had announced itself to me, even before I turned the corner, by its strong smell of raw fish, salt, brine and blood. Outside a weathered shack, wooden boards on trestles were laden with Greenland halibut, wrasse, chunks of cod and strips of *muktuk*, the skin of the narwhal. A sealer in thigh length rubber boots was dragging a skinned seal across a patch of snow, leaving a trail of blood. Men stood around, hands in pockets, talking. The small town atmosphere of this capital city, a peculiar mixture of country village and Wild West frontier town struck me all over again. And I marvelled that this vast country had a population less than what would fit into a football stadium for an English Premier League match on a Saturday afternoon; a country which if placed over a map of Europe of the same scale would stretch from the south of Norway to the coast of North Africa, covering France and most of Germany on the way.

When I reached the National Museum, it was shut. At least a small bookshop nearby was open where I bought a copy of *Instruction in Kayak Building* by H.C. Petersen with text in English, Greenlandic and Danish. Petersen, who was principal of the Knud Rasmussen High School in Sisimiut, set out to learn what he could about traditional ways of kayak construction from the last of the old kayak builders, and put it in a book so that the younger generation would know how to do it. The length of a kayak, he says, should be three times the height of the person it is being made for, and it must fit the hips snugly enough to ensure that the paddler cannot be displaced. Petersen suggests that the traditional sealskin covering is now too expensive and that canvas is a good substitute. He recommends that the canvas is saturated in linseed oil and given two coats of oil paint, preferably white.

John Peterson had previously e-mailed me the rules of the National Kayak Championships. In addition to the usual sprints and long distance races, there were 28 different capsize manoeuvres that could be performed. As well as what we would regard as fairly standard rolls and variations on them, there was rolling with the paddle held in the crook of the elbow, various rolls using a throwing stick (a stick to give leverage when throwing a harpoon) instead of a paddle, and a range of hand rolls, including one with a clenched fist, another using the elbow only, and finally a no-hands roll in which the roll is performed with the arms crossed and pressed against the chest at all times. All of these have their origins in coping with various situations and emergencies while hunting, such as loss of paddle, injury or entanglement. The rules also mentioned something called the Walrus Pull, in which the competitor has to prevent a capsize, while five men on the end of an attached rope pull the kayak sideways from the shore. In the paddling upside down competition you must travel a straight, marked course while capsized. One point is scored for the first three metres and an additional point for each two metres after that.

The rules include a large section on rope gymnastics. These are performed using two ropes slung between poles up to five metres apart. There are 74 set manoeuvres, for example: turning while lying on top of the two ropes; capsize, pick up an object on the ground and roll up again; do a complete loop holding the ropes with forefingers only. The competitor has to perform as many different manoeuvres as he can within 30 minutes. These exercises are designed to strengthen paddlers and develop balance, flexibility, co-ordination and pain tolerance, and to provide training in moving the body and changing the position of the centre of gravity in the same way as in rolling a kayak.

Early in the afternoon, in chilly, overcast conditions, we launched the kayaks into the grey sea and, loaded to the gunwales with excess baggage, distress flares, spare paddle (of the kind that split in half) and a hand pump for pumping out waterlogged boats strapped to our rear decks, headed north into the complex of fjords. Contrary to what some people might think, once they are in the water heavily loaded kayaks are usually easier to handle than unloaded ones. They are not so bouncy and skittish; they lie lower in the water, are more stable and carve through the waves rather than bob up and down over the top of them. And thereby hangs a tale. On a day trip on the west coast of Scotland, carrying little more than our sandwiches, one of our group unbeknown to the rest of us, decided to give ballast and weight to his kayak by filling it with boulders lying at the water's edge. When we returned at the end of the day, he found some reason to dash off in his car on some errand to the nearest village, leaving the rest of us to stagger panting up the long, long beach, arms stretching, backs breaking, knees buckling, too stupid to realize what was going on.

We wore spray decks, which you step into like a waterproof skirt with an elasticated outer edge. This is stretched tightly over the rim of the cockpit once you are seated to keep out spray and breaking waves and, of course, to keep you watertight in the event of a capsize so that you can roll up without shipping water. Another item of apparel we were all wearing was what in North America is known as a PFD (personal flotation device), or a lifejacket. The difference between a lifejacket (or PFD) and a buoyancy aid is that the former is designed to turn a floating body to a face up position, essential for survival if the person is unconscious. Except for Valdemar, for whom this was a perfectly good summer day, we had all chosen to use our paddle mitts or pogies. These are like large gloves with open palms that wrap round the paddle shaft and fasten with velcro. Sliding your hand into the first mitt is easy enough because you have your bare second hand to help, but getting the other hand into its mitt is a job for your teeth. The open palms allow a much better grip on the paddle, and skin contact with the shaft lets all those almost subliminal messages about the precise angle of the blade in the water and the amount of pressure exerted to reach the brain. The rest of me was kept warm by a double thickness windproof cagoule with a hood, a woolly cap, several layers of fleece, waterproof trousers and rubber boots.

All of us had brought with us either wet suits or dry suits. Wet suits keep you warm when immersed in cold water by trapping a thin layer of water between the tight fitting neoprene and your body, which quickly warms up. Dry suits seal at the neck and cuffs and don't let any water in, but unless they are made of very expensive breathable material, you soon get into a muck

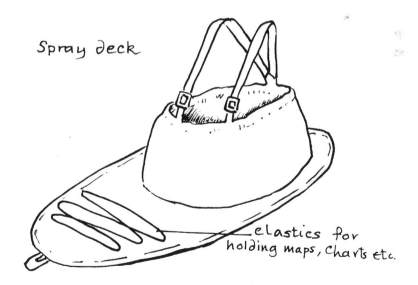

Spray deck

elastics for holding maps, charts etc.

Illustration of spray deck

sweat inside them. Also, both wet and dry suits restrict the arms and make paddling seem like harder work. Although cold water robs the body of its heat 32 times faster than air of the same temperature, each of us had made our own decision to stick to comfier, better-ventilated clothing. In the safety versus comfort dilemma, the deciding factor was probably that we were not paddling in the open sea, but in a sheltered fjord system, never too far from land, and mostly protected from the worst effects of the sudden storms which appear from nowhere in this part of the world.

We paddled in silence, concentrating on discovering the little idiosyncrasies of our kayaks, learning new equations of balance and weight distribution, getting used to the feel of a different paddle in our hands. Once you are used to a particular paddle, it becomes rather like a favourite golf club or cricket bat, just right in the hand, the balance the way you like it, so that you're convinced you won't perform quite so well with any other one. Nuuk disappeared behind a rocky headland. Barren slopes rose steeply into low-lying cloud. According to the map we were surrounded by peaks four or five thousand feet high, but all we saw were waterfalls plunging out of the mist into the fjord. So far, the water was free of ice.

That the day was grey and dull and the view limited didn't matter. I felt a lifting of the heart, an easing of the mind, a refreshing of the spirit as the cares of the everyday world dropped away. I was heading out on a trip I had wanted to do for years, into a land of fantastical and semi-mythical proportions. In a slender craft, in touch with the rhythms of the sea, I was at one with the elements. I was paddling past the oldest known landscape on this planet, past metamorphic rocks nearly four billion years old, laid bare and scraped clean by the action of ice, so that I felt as close to the beginning of time as I was ever likely to be. And the mist and low cloud had their own attractions. As with *The Dance of the Seven Veils*, the occasional revelation of what lay beyond made the scenery all the more exciting. Sometimes the waterfalls slid over slabs of smooth rock, dividing and sub-dividing on the way like a vertical river delta; sometimes they roared down steep, narrow, boulder-strewn valleys or channels before plummeting into the fjord, churning the water into a blue-green froth.

Paddling beside Valdemar I learned that last summer he had crossed the Greenland icecap on skis with a group of Frenchmen. Other Greenlanders had done it with dog sleds, but he was the first Greenlander to do it on skis. An important part of his preparation, he said, had been the mental readiness he achieved by reading of the very first crossing, made in 1888 by the Norwegian Fridtjof Nansen. He too had done it on skis, crossing from east to west. Because cold air sinks and flows downwards off the high plateau of the icecap, the first part of the crossing had been in the face of strong winds, and the last part with the wind at their backs.

Miles of cliffs and waterfalls could be seen on the first few days of paddling

Without warning the wind struck. In seconds the placid sea was whipped into ranks of foaming, fast moving waves. Drenched in spray, we battled to gain the shelter of a cliff girt bay. We landed on a narrow strip of shingle beneath the cliffs. The wind, straight from the icecap, was bitterly cold now that the exertion of paddling no longer warmed us. Up went the large tarpaulin and we huddled in its shelter, soaked and shivering. I recalled reading somewhere that a 20 mph wind at zero degrees Fahrenheit produces greater heat loss than −40°F and no wind. Crouching under that tarpaulin I needed no convincing about the truth of this. We waited for the wind to die down. Clearly it wasn't going to. It was driving a freezing, sleety rain horizontally at us. We decided to set up camp before it got any worse.

And then we encountered a problem that was to recur throughout the trip. Along this precipitous coastline, landing places were few and far between. They tended to be narrow beaches, awash at high tide and backed by steep slopes. We had to unload the kayaks and carry them up a mini cliff. Even unloaded, the heavy canvas doubles required six panting, cursing people to lift them to safety. And then a substantial part of the gear had to be carried another 300 feet up the slope in three lung bursting journeys before any ground flat enough to pitch a tent could be found. At least it got the circulation going again.

But that wasn't the end of it. Trying to erect a tent in a high wind is difficult at the best of times; trying to do it with a tent of unfamiliar design, blinded by sleet, and with hands completely numb is a nightmare. Luckily, Louis, my tent mate, was the soul of patience. While he sorted out the guy ropes, I went in search of boulders. Because the Arctic soil is so thin, often less than an inch in depth before rock or permafrost takes over, the tents had to be anchored by boulders rather than pegs. The trouble was, in acres of empty heath land and barren rock there wasn't a loose boulder in sight. In vain I scoured an area several hundred yards in radius from the wild, billowing thing that was our tent, and to which Louis desperately clung. We had realised too late that we should have kept the tent flat until all the boulders were assembled. At last I spotted a precious hoard in a little lake, beneath the ice. I staggered through the gale from lake to tent, hefting the heavy stones, still soaked to the skin, plunging my arms into the ice choked water on each visit. At last the tent was up and we crawled into it to change into dry clothes and spread out our air mattresses and sleeping bags.

Meanwhile, Joan, Cathy and Valdemar had a meal on the go under the tarp. We crowded together for warmth. How I wished I had brought a folding chair with me that would have raised my bum off the cold ground and enabled me to lean back instead of sit upright on a hard storage bottle. At that point I was wearing, from the skin outwards, a thermal long-sleeved vest, then another one of double thickness, a long-sleeved silk vest, a thick fleece jacket, a heavy-weight, waist-length kayaking cagoule and, on top of that, a knee-length Gore-Tex jacket — and I was only just warm enough!

It was too cold to hang about being sociable. Immediately after the meal we retired to our tents and to the warmth of our sleeping bags. It struck me that it would be on days such as this or during the long winter night that the Inuit passed the time with their string games. As a child I learned to make a simple string figure called a Cat's Cradle. The Inuit, however, could make many hundreds of figures of animals, fish, birds and humans from memory, some of which could be made to move to illustrate stories that were told at the same time. Some of the figures were too complicated to be worked by fingers alone, so that toes, teeth and even noses had to be pressed into service, or they were operated by teams of two or three people. The most complicated figures took years to learn and were mastered only by a few Inuit. *Ajarraaq*, as the Inuit call it, is now a dying art. When I looked up string games on the Internet, I discovered that there were well over a hundred sites devoted to it, as well as magazines, clubs and competitions. I had stumbled on a kind of sub-culture that I'd had no idea existed. String games seem to have been fairly common to hunter-gatherer societies throughout the world. It used to be said that the most useful piece of equipment an anthropologist could take on a field study was a bit of string.

As we lay listening to the humming of the guy ropes and the splutter of hail and rain upon the fabric of the tent, I told Louis about other experiences I'd had of high winds, about a hike in the Scottish mountains when I'd seen a mighty up-draught stop a waterfall in mid plunge, hurling it upwards in a mass of flying spray. I told him about being caught out at sea in my kayak in a force 9 gale. Six of us were camping on the Garvellach Isles on Scotland's west coast. We knew the wind was strong, but overconfidence and male pride led us into making the bad mistake of setting out. The seven-mile crossing back to Easdale on the mainland would not have taken much more than an hour and a half on a calm day. In the first hour, paddling into the teeth of the gale, up and down and through gigantic waves, I moved forward barely 100 yards. The enemy was not the sea. The enemy was fear, cold, fatigue and loneliness. And the greatest of these was loneliness, for the storm had scattered the group, so that, for long stretches at a time, nobody else was in sight. In the third and fourth hours of paddling I entered uncharted mental states, plunging from pure joy into troughs of terror and despair, going from screaming with rage at my kayak for not keeping straight, to singing at the top of my voice with sheer exhilaration at the power, the splendour, the magnificence of the mighty ocean.

Finally, in the fifth hour, totally exhausted, I reached Easdale. One of the others who had landed ahead of me opened his car door. The wind wrenched it off its hinges and sent it scudding across the tarmac car park like a leaf until it crumpled against a wall. Louis was very quiet, no doubt deeply impressed by my adventure, I thought, until a loud snore told me otherwise.

Still with most of my clothes on I wriggled deep into my Arctic sleeping bag, adding my breath to my body heat to raise the temperature inside my cocoon. My pillow was my lifejacket wrapped around a bag of clothes. I lay, knees drawn up, savouring warmth and snugness while the cold prowled outside, recalling those freezing nights at boarding school in winter; a long, unheated, draughty dormitory, windows wide open by order, one thin, regulation blanket.

'Bonjour, Louis.'

'Bonjour, Robin.'

During the night the wind had howled, the rain lashed and the call of nature grew steadily more insistent. I confessed to Louis that, rather than crawl out of the tent, I had used one of his welly boots. Actually, foreseeing this problem, I had brought a wide necked, screw top bottle with me. But thereafter, the first thing Louis did every morning was to peer into his boots with deep suspicion.

At least the freezing wind had dropped. Grey mist hung over grey, wet rock and sullen grey sea. I retrieved my clothes from the bottom of my sleeping bag. Several hours of body heat had turned them from wet to merely damp. I dragged them on, my flesh cringing in protest.

'Just remember, Louis, we're doing this for enjoyment,' I said.

Whether to have a sleeping bag of down or of synthetic fibres is one of those arguments guaranteed to split any normally paranoid, partisan and prejudiced group of kayakers into snarling factions. Hesitantly, therefore, I claim one advantage of synthetic fibre to be that, unlike down, a soaking does not adversely affect its insulating properties.

My notes, scrawled in my diary or journal (a humble school jotter, in fact), record that 'the tent bit me'. Which is to say, in taking it down, one of the collapsible spring-loaded hoops snapped back at me, gouging a chunk of flesh from my thumb. Sore muscles, cut thumb, diarrhoea, and it's only day two.

The warmest place in these conditions is the kayak, the lower half of one's body being snugly enclosed while the top half glows with the effort of paddling. Those with Arctic experience, however, advised against starting until the mist showed signs of thinning. In these parts the compass needle deviates from true north by about 35 degrees and seems to vary from one fjord to another, so that navigation by compass is unreliable. To lose sight of the shore could have serious consequences and, furthermore, there was always the possibility of icebergs lurking in the mist. So it was nearly midday before we launched, but not before we had reversed the exhausting process of humping all our gear and supplies and the kayaks back down the steep slope to the narrow beach. As we rapidly learned on this expedition, you got into the kayaks for a rest.

Yesterday we had been in a sudden storm and capsize might well have occurred, considering that one or two in the group were not regular paddlers and hadn't quite got back into the swing of things. The sea temperature was a bit below 40°F (less than 4°C), which, in theory at least, should allow most reasonably fit people about 20 minutes in the water before becoming unconscious and maybe one hour before death. Further north in Greenland, and earlier in the year, the survival time in the water is reckoned to be about three minutes.

I had discovered that I was in a minority in being able to roll a kayak. I am talking about a single kayak. Our matronly canvas doubles were almost impossible to roll. Even sleeker, fibreglass models are extremely difficult to roll and need a lot of practice by the two paddlers involved to ensure that their movements are co-ordinated. Therefore, team rescue techniques would be called for in the event of capsize. The usual method is for two or more kayaks to form a raft on either side of the upturned boat. One of the rescuers then flips the capsized boat upright. While someone empties the flooded boat with a hand pump, the one who has gone for a swim works his or her way back into the cockpit, feet first, with one leg over the stern of the empty kayak and one leg over one of the rescue kayaks alongside it. It takes practice and working as a team to do this properly. After a few training sessions though, it should be possible to get someone back in their boat inside three or four minutes. The majority of the others had gathered for a training weekend a few weeks prior to arriving in Greenland. Much to everyone's relief, our leaders decided that since I was an instructor who taught rescue techniques to others, it would not be necessary to go through the drills again for my benefit.

Sermitsiaq Island, along whose bare, precipitous coast we paddled had its own mini icecap from which melt water tumbled into the fjord in a series of ever more spectacular waterfalls. We began to encounter the first small icebergs, each about the size of an armchair or a car, the remains of the giants which the glacier had calved a hundred kilometres to the east and which had slowly drifted down the fjord system on tide and current towards the open sea, diminishing in size, day by day. The gradual depletion of the icebergs is caused by evaporation, and by the constant attack of the waves that undercut their sides causing bits to collapse into the sea just as happens through the erosion of coastal cliffs. Icebergs might also scrape along the sea bed or run aground, breaking off underwater chunks, or collide with each other; something which

The first small icebergs began to appear

usually occurs below the waterline since about seven eighths of an iceberg is submerged.

These eroded shapes were like crystal swans, white galleons in full sail, or translucent sculptures sliding from one shape to another. I clicked away with my camera, producing amused smiles from the old hands who kept assuring me that, in a day or two, I'd wonder why on earth I'd bothered with these tiddlers. Reaching out, I broke off a small piece. As it melted in my mouth I reflected that the last time it had been liquid was 15,000 years ago and it still tasted as fresh as any spring water. One particularly beautiful glass flower enfolded an emerald lake. Unable to resist, I glided between the ice petals and out the other side. Seconds later it shuddered, bubbled and turned over. Had I been trapped beneath it I would surely have drowned. From then on, all of us treated even the little bergs with great respect.

The glaciers that terminate on Greenland's west coast produce the majority of the Northern Hemisphere's icebergs. Estimates of the number of icebergs calving from these glaciers vary from 10,000 to 40,000 a year, of which an average of 300 to 400 float south of Newfoundland into the North Atlantic shipping lanes where they become a navigational hazard. The largest Northern Hemisphere iceberg on record was sighted near Baffin Island in 1882, 13 kilometres long, 6 kilometres wide and about 20 metres above the waterline. Someone calculated that it contained enough fresh water for everyone in the world to drink a litre a day for four years. Iceberg water has, in fact, become a marketable commodity. Icebergs from the North Atlantic are towed into Newfoundland, melted down and bottled. Untouched by the elements of today, the water is free of pesticides, herbicides and pollutants, and is marketed as 'nature's purest water on the planet'.

Recently I was kayaking in Hawaii (open kayaks with no top deck, shorts, t-shirt, bare feet – talk about going from one extreme to the other!) and learned that bottled, desalinated deep seawater is likely to become Hawaii's number one export if demand for it in Japan continues. One small bottle sells at over $30. Water is brought up from a depth of 2,000 feet by a pipe. At these depths it contains various minerals and salts not found nearer the surface and is also free from the products of photosynthesis. It is claimed that deep seawater aids weight loss, and improves skin tone and digestion.

We paddled at a leisurely pace for eight hours with two breaks, one of an hour and one of half an hour, covering about 25 miles. For the last few hours the mist cleared and the sun glinted on snow slopes out of which rose peaks and spires so fantastically pointed that they must surely have been the abode of the Snow Queen or the Wizard of the North. The last couple of miles, crossing from Sermitsiaq Island to our campsite on an island with the Inuit name of *Qornup Qeqertarassua*, was done in a brisk cross-wind with waves slapping at us sideways, drenching us in spray.

We landed at ten in the evening. The bay was sheltered from the wind, which meant the mosquitoes and little black flies or 'no-see-ums' were out in force. These bugs are a fact of life in the Arctic Summer. Stagnant pools or boggy heath, which cannot drain because of the rock or permafrost beneath, make ideal breeding conditions for mosquitoes and other critters of that ilk with kamikaze intent. In many Inuit dialects, July is known as 'mosquito month'. Eskimos used to wear mosquito nets made from the long guard hairs of musk oxen and they burnt smouldering leaves in smudge pots in their tents. There are many accounts of the early explorers and prospectors being tormented to the point of hysteria and insanity by this black horde. For a long time it was not known why some herds of Canadian caribou occasionally made a double migration, moving south in the middle of the summer, returning, and then leaving the tundra again at the onset of winter. It is now thought that they do this in the years when the bugs have multiplied in particularly large numbers, making life unbearable for them. For the same reason, exposed and windy promontories are favoured gathering places for caribou.

Anyway, the first thing we did on landing was to pull on our bug hats. These are similar to what beekeepers wear; fine netting suspended from a hat and tucked in at the neck. There is a whole range of bug repelling sprays and lotions on the market, of course, but when the enemy are dive bombing you in their trillions, a physical barrier between you and them seems imperative. Some of our group had bug jackets. These are hooded garments made of what looks like cotton waste. You shove the thing into an airtight container along with some incredibly powerful fluid. When the jacket has absorbed this, you take it out and put it on. I'm not sure whether it repels the bugs, but it certainly repels all fellow campers. After a bit you got so used to wearing a bug hat you didn't notice it was there. I was forever trying to push food into my mouth only to find the net in the way. Worse still was when I spat or blew my nose.

'Rub dry cigarette ash into the bites, it's very soothing,' someone once advised me, adding, 'unless it's still smouldering'. Soon after returning from Greenland I was out paddling with a couple of friends on Loch Goil on the west coast of Scotland. At the lunch break on a beach they started flapping their hands and cursing, saying the midges were exceptionally bad here. I hadn't even noticed them.

'What's the national bird of Greenland, Robin?'

'I don't know, Heather, what is it?'

'The mosquito!'

Well, it seemed funny at the time.

What had looked like reasonably flat ground from the water was a mass of small bumps and hummocks. With difficulty Louis and I located a small patch where our hips and ribs, if nothing else, might be placed with only minor discomfort. Obviously the others were experiencing similar problems for the tents were scattered over an area of about half a square mile. Clothes lay spread over rock and bush or draped across tents in a vain attempt to dry them, but even when the sun shines things dry very slowly at this latitude.

As always, though, the big tarpaulin was the focus of the group, and there, at midnight, we ate our main meal of the day.

There was still enough light for me to take a photograph of the scene, a full moon hanging in a pale blue sky, the snow tinged with pink as the sun sank behind the mountains. Exactly when the sun disappeared each day depended on where we were in relation to the mountains, their configuration and height and so on. One thing never varied though — the amazing speed with which the temperature plummeted once the direct rays of the sun were cut off. On some days we would go from feeling comfortable in nothing but a t-shirt (bugs permitting) to needing four or five layers of clothing, in less than ten minutes.

Time has a different meaning when the light never really fades. And the same goes for when there are four or five months of darkness. Perhaps things are a bit more regulated now, but in the old days of the gold rushes in Alaska and the Yukon, people simply followed their own schedules. In my novel, *The Dreamhouse,* I tried to depict what it was like when it was 'night all night in the day time' by having two stores, side by side in the main street of a mining town, one displaying a sign, 'Out to Lunch,' the other with a sign, 'Closed for the Night.' Those kids playing football outside the seaman's hostel in Nuuk at three in the morning didn't seem so strange after all. There are times when one's biological clock can go very wrong, as I discovered once when on a four day solo hike across the Cairngorms. On the first day I lost my watch. It was midsummer, with almost continual daylight. I must have been getting up at two or three in the morning, thinking it was about nine. On the last day, I came tearing down the hill with a raging thirst, hoping I'd make it to the pub before the bar closed for the night. When I got there, it was closed ... because they didn't open till five-thirty and it was only three in the afternoon.

We sat in the shelter of the tarp, squeezed together for warmth, discussing the word 'day.' If it is defined by light and dark, then at the poles there is a six month day, followed by a six month night, but if a day is defined as the time it takes for a planet to spin on its axis and a year is the time taken to revolve around its sun, there are plenty of planets where a day is longer than a year.

The talk turned to other trips and expeditions we had done. I soon realised that, although I might be the most experienced kayaker there, I was the least experienced in Arctic conditions. Several had paddled the Nahanni River, a tributary of the Mackenzie, which swirls through spectacular gorges; others spoke of backpacking in the Yukon and in the mountain ranges of Baffin Island, of the Hood River, jewel of the Barrens, of the Peel River Reserve and of the Ingraham Trail. For Heather, this was her seventh Arctic summer.

Listening to these Canadians talk about the Northwest Territories and the High Arctic, I caught something of the spirit of Robert Service — he who, in *The Shooting of Dan McGrew* and *The Cremation of Sam McGee*, captured the lure of the north:

> *There are strange things done*
> *In the midnight sun*
> *By men who moil for gold;*
> *The Arctic trails have their secret tales*
> *That would make your blood run cold.*

I began to appreciate the vastness of the Canadian wilderness and how much adventure still awaited me. For my part, I spoke of the Outer Hebrides, the Corryvreckan whirlpool, of booming sea caves, the magic of the Treshnish Isles, of places with music in their Gaelic names and of Tir Nan Og, perpetually just beyond the horizon, the Land of the Ever Young.

Back in our tent, Louis asked me why I'd come on this trip. I said I had wanted to experience unspoiled nature – well, comparatively unspoiled nature. I wanted to get away from landing on a beach and finding rusty beer cans and assorted bits of plastic. I wanted to walk over country where there were no 'Keep Out' notices, no well-worn paths or sign-posted routes. Once, in Switzerland, I told Louis, I'd had to wait in a queue on a mountainside for my turn to step onto the summit. It was ironic, we agreed, that the presence of our group here, no matter how careful we were, was contributing to an inexorable slide towards these very things we abhorred. Pioneers and explorers, drawn to the wilderness, inevitably carry with them the seeds of destruction of the thing they love.

I told Louis how, in my last year at school, I'd been enthralled by an account of the two expeditions to Greenland in the 1930s led by Gino Watkins. Gino and one of his companions, Freddy Spencer Chapman had become my heroes. It was partly their youth that captured my imagination. Gino had sufficiently impressed the hierarchy of the Royal Geographical Society with previous explorations in Spitsbergen and Labrador for them to back his plans for Greenland despite the fact that he was then only twenty-three. 'A man should achieve everything he wants in life by the time he's twenty-five,' Gino is reported to have said. Gino and his companions were the first Britons to learn to roll a kayak and to hunt seals from them, Eskimo style. On the second expedition Gino met his death. He was just twenty-five. He set out alone in his kayak to hunt seals. Later, his kayak was found, swamped and adrift. His trousers and spray skirt were found on a small ice floe some distance away. Was he capsized by the recoil of his gun or, perhaps, by a wave from a calving glacier? Did he land on the ice floe only for his kayak to slip away? It is possible that he took his trousers off to try to extend his reach in a desperate attempt to retrieve the kayak. Or did he make the fatal error of attempting to swim after it? We will never know exactly what happened.

At Cambridge, youthful fantasies of following in my heroes' footsteps were fuelled by the knowledge that they had both been students there. At that time Cambridge was the furthest north I'd ever been in my life. A fellow member of the Cambridge University Mountaineering Club regaled me with accounts of climbing in a magical place where it never got dark in the summer and where it was possible to read a newspaper at midnight.

Louis stirred in his sleeping bag.

'He'd been to the Arctic then?'

'No. The place was called Scotland.'

Next morning, the mist was back again. According to map and guide book, just over the hill on the next promontory was the site of a Viking settlement. Clearly Tom had anticipated this months ahead and had prepared 'a little talk'. And clearly, feathers were going to be ruffled, feelings hurt and professional pride dented ('the worst thing you can do to your dignity is to stand on it,' a wise aunt once told me) if we did not all assemble on the site within the next ten minutes. Grumpily we trudged across a boggy hillside to the windswept promontory and huddled in a small depression lined with turf and surrounded by large leaved plants akin to wild rhubarb.

Here and there bits of stone wall protruded. This, announced Tom, had been the main room and on the other side of the wall was where the outhouse and cattle byre had been. At some time, probably in the 11th or 12th century a Viking family had lived there. The thick stone walls would have been insulated and roofed with turf and the roof beams were most probably made of imported timber This was the height of summer and the place was cold, barren and treeless. It hadn't always been like that, Tom said. In the 13th century, there was a dramatic change in the climate of these latitudes. Before then, the southerly limit of the sea ice was some two or three hundred miles north of its present position and, likewise, the forests extended much further north than they do today. In those earlier centuries, there was good grazing to be had in southern Greenland. I tried to imagine the scene inside this room with perhaps the women carding, spinning and weaving wool while an old man related a saga. After a hard winter, the cattle were so weak and unexercised they had to be carried out to the fields: not as difficult a thing to do as one might think because the Norse breeds of yesteryear were much smaller than they are these days.

In the year 982, Erik the Red was banished from Iceland for three years for killing several people in a feud. With his family, his retainers, thralls and chattels, he sailed westwards in search of the new land he'd heard about. In the Nuuk fjordlands, Erik found rich pasturage for his livestock and discovered herds of reindeer to provide meat and hides. Having served his three years of banishment, Erik returned to Iceland, spread the good news about the land he had named Greenland, gathered together 25 ships and returned with some 500 people who settled in the south and in the Nuuk fjords. The latter was called the Western Settlement or Vesterbyden. This was where we were now, in one of the farmsteads of Vesterbyden. At one point there were about 90 Viking farms dotted around the shores of these fjords. As far as is known, relations with the Inuit or *Skraelings*, as the Norsemen called them, were, if not amicable, at least not overtly hostile. The Norse word *skraeling* means 'wretch' or 'savage', although it seems that the material culture of the Inuit and their standard of living was every bit as high as those of the Norsemen who affected to despise them.

The two settlements, the westernmost outpost of Christianity and European culture in the Middle Ages, formed a thriving, self-governing republic, trading with northern Europe in sealskins, polar bear hides, gyrfalcons and walrus ivory: the latter being the only source of ivory in Medieval Europe.

Norse manuscript records the standard sailing directions of those days for a voyage direct from Norway to Greenland:

'From Norway one should sail constantly westward to Wharf (Cape Farewell?) in Greenland. The route is north of the Shetlands in such a way that they can be seen only under good conditions of visibility; but one passes so far south of the Faroe Islands that the horizon is mid way up the mountain sides. One passes at the right distance south of Iceland so that its birds and whales are met with.'

From the western fjords of Greenland, the Vikings went on to explore Baffin Island and much of the coast of Labrador and Newfoundland, but that's another story. Then began a decline until, by 1350, the Norse Greenlanders of the Western Settlement had all died out or departed, and homesteads, such as the one in which I sat shivering, lay abandoned.

The lecture was over. I ran down the hill, pulling on my bug hat as the black horde fell upon me in the sheltered lower slopes. They didn't have long to wait. As I squatted with my trousers down, behind the same big boulder I'd already visited twice before that morning, they feasted for a third time on my exposed flesh, unable to believe their luck. Perhaps the Vikings left because they couldn't stand the bugs a moment longer.

I was careful to ensure that where I squatted was below the high water mark. 'Everything we bring in we carry out again,' was the rule. And that included our own bodily waste matter, unless we chose to go below the high water mark. Canadians in general seem to be very environmentally aware. In Toronto, for instance, smoking is forbidden anywhere except in private homes and it's an offence to leave your car engine running for more than a minute if you are stationary. Everyone in the group, except me, had read the book, *How to Shit in the Woods*. When I first heard of it, I thought it must be some kind of joke book. It's not. It deals with topics like the rate human faeces deteriorates in different climatic conditions, how to avoid contaminating water supplies and the merits of different biodegradable toilet papers. So, unless we were prepared to clamber amongst slippery boulders at the waterline, we had to head inland armed with a self-sealing green bag and a shovel. In order not to contaminate our food, all the garbage, after being bagged, went into one double kayak. 'The garbage boat' as it was called, was the one paddled by Tom and Carol, the two Americans.

'Which just about expresses,' said Carol, 'What you Canadians think of your southern neighbours.'

Unlike the other kayaks, which got lighter as the days went by, the garbage boat got heavier, but thankfully not smellier, since the seals on the bags were super efficient.

Icebergs becoming larger
(courtesy of Chuck Copeland)

We embarked on another long paddle, directly into a biting wind that funnelled down the fjord, straight from the icecap. After about an hour of paddling my hands were frozen, despite my Arctic mitts, and my feet had lost all feeling even though I had put an insulating mat at the point where my feet were in contact with the thin hull. It started to rain again. We were now beginning to encounter bigger icebergs. Their sheer beauty and variety lifted my mind above a host of bodily discomforts. Circle an iceberg and every angle offers new, unsuspected miracles of geometry. Some, like sapphires in the mist, were astonishing in the way they radiated blue; others slid almost imperceptibly from a white so sharp it hurt the eyes, to the deep, deep blueness of the caves along their waterline.

The bluest icebergs were the ones that had recently turned over. The age of the ice, the degree of compression, its crystalline structure, the presence of air bubbles, the amount of salt water absorbed by the ice, the extent of melting and refreezing, all these things have a bearing on the way the ice refracts and reflects light. For instance, some of the icebergs we passed were streaked with veins of blue or green. These were former crevasses in the glacier that now varied in colour according to whether they had subsequently filled with rainwater, melt-water, or seawater. Their fantastic shapes were partly the action of wind and of evaporation, but mostly, they seemed to be the result of capsizing. The sea undercuts them at the waterline, creating sharp edges, hollows and runnels. When the berg rolls over, these rise into the air, presenting ice wings and ridged forms to the sky. Then the process starts again and, on each capsize, the berg arises transformed, more amazing, more unbelievable than before.

Trying to keep warm I sprinted past the double containing Guylaine and her partner, Marc Lebeau. He was almost blue with cold.

'You've heard of Eric the Red,' I shouted. 'Now meet Marc the Blue!'

The answer was a drumming of feet. I knew the sound. I'd tried it myself to get the feeling back into the toes. I slowed and kept pace with them. Talking always helps to pass the miles, so I talked of those who had preceded the Vikings. In the 5th and 6th centuries the monasteries of Ireland were the centres of high culture in Europe. From Ireland monks ventured north and west to establish cells and monasteries in the Faeroes and in Iceland. The Arctic explorer, Vilhjalmur Steffansson had great respect for these monks. In his opinion, the New World was discovered by whoever discovered Iceland. To reach Iceland a voyager must cross a wide and stormy ocean far out of sight of land, but, after that, it is possible to see westward from island to island till the mainland of North America rises above the horizon.

Perhaps, though, others had preceded the Irish monks. It is just possible, for example, that Pytheas, the astronomer and geographer of the Greek colony of Marsala (Marseilles), came this way sometime in the 5th or 6th century AD. He wrote an account, *Peri ton Okeanon (About the Ocean)* of his journeys north beyond Gibraltar to find sources of cassiterite and elektron (tin and amber). Some scholars think it was either Iceland or Norway he was describing, but he certainly encountered sea ice. Other early Greek and Roman writers and geographers make reference to his account. However, some time during the 6th or 7th century, during the destruction of the Great Library of Alexandria, the manuscript disappeared. All that is known about it now is what others say about it. That the marine technology and navigation skills existed to make such a voyage is believable. In the 4th century BC, Herodotus tells of the three-year long Phoenician circumnavigation of Africa, from east to west, in about 600 BC (some 2,000 years before Bartholomew Diaz rounded the Cape of Good Hope from west to east).

We caught up with the flagging Tom and Carol.

Carol said, 'The Vikings must have rowed or sailed their long-ships up this fjord'.

Tom informed us that the words 'port' and 'starboard' derived from the Viking long-ships. A large flat paddle called a steer board, which was always on the right hand side, was used as a rudder. When the long-ship reached port, it docked with the other side against the quay to avoid damaging the steer board.

We speculated about whether the Black Death ever reached Greenland. Tom thought not. Indeed, by that date, contact with Europe was minimal. A more likely explanation for the disappearance of the Vikings from these shores was, he thought, the southward creep of Arctic conditions. Analysis of Viking bones showed a decline in health and evidence of famine in the later years. When the Vikings converted to Christianity, the Church had forbidden contact with the heathen Inuit. This might have caused a decline in the Vikings' hunting skills and also in their ability to trade meat with the Inuit, thus contributing to the food shortage brought on by the mini Ice Age.

'And then there was the union with Norway in 1260 something.' Tom was now plying his paddle with a vigour equal to his enthusiasm for his subject. Carol threw me a grateful glance. The Vikings were carrying us down the fjord.

'Remind me about that treaty,' I said innocently, and learned that it had given Norway a monopoly of trade with Greenland. But they neglected this trade, and essentials needed to support the Greenland communities became a mere trickle.

'For Heaven's sake don't use that word, Tom! I'm dying for a pee!'

'You'll be lucky!'

'Hey, Louis! Chuck your welly boot over!'

We hauled out for what came to be known as a 'bladder break' and a brew up on a sloping slab of rock, the only possible landing place for miles, which bore long furrows as if a giant tiger had raked it with its claws. The main Ice Age, which had scoured this land like a giant file 8–12,000 years ago, had picked the landscape clean, leaving only the Earth's ancient, bare bones. All around, steep, dark-blue mountains ringed a slate sea, which made the icebergs seem all the whiter. I had been told I'd find this part of Greenland in July like the Scottish hills in March. If I ignored the icebergs and the fact that everything was bigger and steeper, I could see a vague likeness. There were large snowfields everywhere, but not a complete covering, and there was low cloud and mist. We hopped about, stamped our feet and flapped our arms. In this, Greenland's warmest month, I was as cold, if not colder than I'd ever been on any Scottish mountaintop in winter.

Close by was a fox trap, a small cell constructed from stones. Above the entrance a large slab was suspended on a string, ready to be tripped when the fox entered to snatch the bait. The foxes are trapped for their furs. In winter their fur is entirely white, and in summer the coat ranges from grey to brown. They hunt wild duck, lemmings and Arctic voles, and also seek out birds' eggs and carrion. In the summer months when food is plentiful, Arctic foxes collect a surplus and store it in their dens. In lean years they will eat insects and berries. The Arctic fox is smaller than the red fox, with shorter legs, tail and ears and a blunter nose, all means of minimising heat loss.

In the search for Sir John Franklin in the Canadian high Arctic, a certain Captain Horatio Austin came up with the idea of trapping foxes then setting them free, having fixed them with metal information tags directing the Franklin party to the search ships and to food caches which had been set out for them. Some of the foxes, it seems, were quietly dispatched by Horatio Austin's sailors, who recognised both a valuable fur and a wacky plan when they saw one.

'It wasn't all a one-way traffic,' I said to Tom when we resumed paddling. 'There's evidence of a few Inuit reaching Scotland in their kayaks.'

Glad of something to keep my mind off the biting wind, I told him about the selkies of Orkney folklore, seal-like creatures that could shed their skins and walk as men. Whether or not these selkies were really Eskimos in kayaks is impossible to say, but there are more solid accounts of what were known as fin-men. Here is the Reverend James Wallace, Minister of Kirkwall in the Orkneys, writing towards the end of the 17th century:

'Sometime about this country I see those men which are called fin-men. In the year 1682 one was seen sometimes sailing, sometimes rowing up and down in his little boat at the south end of the isle. Most people of the isle flocked to see him and when they ventured to put a boat out to see if they could apprehend him, he presently fled away most swiftly. And in the year 1684 another was seen from Westray. And for a while after they got fewer or no fishes, for they have this remark here that the fin-men drive away the fishes from the place to which they come.'

The Reverend Wallace's son, who edited a new edition of his father's memoirs, added that the fin-men's boats were made of sealskin. 'And when in a storm he seeth the high surging of a wave, he has a way of sinking his boat till the wave passeth over.'

In 1760, another reverend, Francis Gatrell, records a sighting in the River Don at Aberdeen, of a canoe seven yards long and two feet wide with a man in it 'who was over all hairy and spoke a language which no person could interpret. He lived but three days though all possible care was taken to recover him.'

This very kayak can be seen today in the Anthropological Museum of Aberdeen University. The design of the craft places it as having come from the same waters in which we were now paddling.

'How could anyone paddle all the way from Greenland?' Carol wanted to know.

'Personally, I need a break after two or three hours of paddling. How could someone, even driven by a storm, paddle ... what ... two or three weeks non-stop?'

We speculated about this. Perhaps they became lost in fog while out hunting, or drifted a great deal further than they realised on ice floes and, paddling eastwards, thought they were returning to the west coast of Greenland. Remembering that the 16th and 17th centuries experienced what was almost another mini Ice Age, it is possible that they found icebergs in mid ocean on which to haul out and rest. Dutch and Scandinavian whalers and traders were in the habit of kidnapping Eskimos, often lifting them out of the sea while still in their kayaks. So another possibility is that the Scottish sightings were of escaping Inuit trying to make it back to Greenland.

'And also, we Greenland guys are pretty tough!' came Valdemar's voice from behind us.

Since he'd paddled quite happily the whole day without mitts or gloves, we heartily agreed.

'I wonder if any of them ever made it back to here.' Tom mused.

We thought it unlikely. Not only was it against the prevailing wind and current, but also Eskimo oral tradition has proved to be both accurate and enduring and there are no tales of this kind.

Several months later, I discussed these things with Stephen Loring, an anthropologist at the Smithsonian Institute in Washington. He said one reason why very long kayak journeys would be difficult to make was that skin boats such as kayaks need to be dried out regularly in order to keep the skins taut over the frames. This is why nearly every coastal Inuit community had special racks onto which the kayaks were lifted as soon as they came out of the water. He recounted how he had recently read a paper by a Russian anthropologist, announcing, in great excitement, the discovery of an unsuspected whale-worshipping cult amongst certain Siberian coastal tribes. In an abandoned settlement, rows of whale skulls with mysterious holes bored into them had been found, between which the villagers must have danced. Stephen said one look at the photographs told him they were, in fact, drying racks minus their slats. On the other hand, he went on to say, excavations had unearthed 18th century skeletons of male Inuit beside those of Russian sailors. The thickness of the Russians' humerus, the bone that carries the biceps and triceps, compared to that of the Inuits' was like the difference between a matchstick and a broom handle. Although this evidence comes from the Aleutian Eskimos, it does suggest that the Greenlanders of those days might have had the physical strength to paddle long distances.

Our campsite was towards the north end of Qeqertarsuaq Island, at the foot of a mountain of about 4,500 feet, or so I surmised from the map since the actual mountain was hidden in mist. We overlooked a bay into which wind and tide had pushed a whole fleet of icebergs. Behind us, scree slopes disappeared into vaporous layers and a mountain torrent thundered over a series of waterfalls: terrain that involved carrying the kayaks and our gear up a long, extremely steep slope. Four of us staggered panting up the slope, a double kayak cradled in webbing slings to which we were harnessed. I focused my mind on the nice rest to come once the kayaks were all lifted to safety.

A rest? I'd forgotten about the boulder-collecting routine.

'Your rocks aren't as big as Valdemar's,' Louis complained, a remark that caused great hilarity amongst the happy campers.

Marc stripped to the waist and washed in the roaring stream. As for me, I watched from the comfort of my six layers of clothing. But soon my eyes were drawn back to the hypnotic icebergs. In the middle of some task, we'd find ourselves standing quite still, turned towards the bay, spellbound by what we saw.

That night in the tarp, with a good hot meal inside us and mugs of cocoa in our hands, I unveiled a spoof Viking saga I had been composing in my head. The old parchment, I claimed, had been authenticated by Professor Tom Burnt-Socks as a genuine Viking document from Greenland, typical of the little-known group called the Gastrofroths:

'This parchment is part of the saga of Robin Little Rocks. Why he was so called is not known. It seems that this saga is now closely linked to that of Louis and the Magic Boot that recounts how, every night, a boot was magically filled with a golden fluid, the elixir of life. Not much is known about the Gastrofroths. Experts, for instance, are still puzzling over the strange ritual in which the elders of the tribe would suddenly leap from their craft and race towards the largest boulders on the shore with cries of ecstasy. Here now is one of the surviving fragments from this precious parchment:

"Oh, we're the daring Gastrofroths, hardier than the Norse,

From whom never is heard a four-letter word ...

Except from Heather, of course...'"

I am not sure that I entirely succeeded in holding my audience who kept turning to look at the icebergs in the bay, overawed, as if in the presence of something from another world. 'Fallen pieces of the Moon' is how Barry Lopez described the icebergs in his book *Arctic Dreams*.

Miles of cliffs, waterfalls and small icebergs

The first few days of paddling

Communal life in 'the tarp'

Ancient scoured rocks

Icebergs becoming bigger and more frequent

A freezing cold beach

Winged bergs sculpted by erosion (courtesy of Ken Nicol)

Dwarfed by ice cliffs on land and sea
(courtesy of Ken Nicol)

A day for sun block – but who's complaining?

Clear skies and sparkling ice

A still and misty day

Sweeping snowfields and jagged ridges (courtesy of Ken Nicol)

A rocky coastline typical of southwest Greenland
(courtesy of Ken Nicol)

The base of the glacier (courtesy of Chuck Copeland)

Mountains catching the late evening sun

Worn ribs of a boat

Arctic flowers (courtesy of Heather Boswell)

Kayaks – traditional and modern – excite young Greenlanders
(courtesy of Ken Nicol)

A beautiful campsite

Underneath the arches, Greenland style (courtesy of Ken Nicol)

Arctic flowers (courtesy of Heather Boswell)

Lunch stop!

Spectacular mountains on the run home

Morning cloud banners (courtesy of Marc Lebeau)

Ocean of Serenity

I didn't need to unzip the tent to know it was another cold, misty morning. From years of kayaking in Scotland I'd run foul of several little known sub-clauses to Sod's Law, like the one which decrees that no matter how much you eat, there's always something that won't fit back into your kayak when you come to repack it; or the one which ensures that, when you need to consult your map, you're bound to be located on the fold. And now I discovered another clause — anything hung up to dry ends up wetter than it started (even if it's inside your tent). There were numerous markers on this trip, such as the point at which we were half way round in miles, or in estimated number of days. But none was more important than the awful moment, different for each of us, when the bag containing the wet clothes grew bigger than the bag with the dry clothes. As we introduced yesterday's damp vests to our shrinking bodies, I told Louis my favourite of the original 33 clauses of Sod's Law: if you see light at the end of a long, dark tunnel, it's bound to be an express train coming towards you.

'Did you hear that noise last night?' Louis asked.

'Like an avalanche? Several times.'

I poked my head out of the tent and gasped, unable to comprehend what I saw. The same bergs were there in more or less the same places and yet they were utterly transformed. I thought I knew what everyone knew, that nine-tenths of an iceberg is underwater, which should make it just about the most stable thing afloat. And yet a large number of the bergs in our bay had capsized. I learned later that this nine-tenths thing is only partly true. The ratio of above and below the waterline can be whittled down to one to one, or to top-heavy proportions by contact with warmer patches of water, by large chunks breaking off underwater, or simply by running aground when there's an outgoing tide. Whatever the reason, the bergs, now the size of bungalows, houses and small ships, were unstable.

Breakfast under the tarp was a shivering, monosyllabic affair, each person wrapped in his or her own thoughts and discomforts.

'Look!' someone shouted.

One of the biggest bergs in the bay was starting to rock and growl and gradually to lean to one side. Like an ocean liner slipping beneath the waves or a slow motion film of a whale turning onto its belly, it rolled over in a welter of bubbles, plumes of spray and hissings of trapped air. Up heaved the gigantic blue underside, a new island emerging from the sea, roaring into existence as water cascaded from it. A wave swept across the bay, setting the neighbouring icebergs in motion so that they groaned and creaked with internal stresses and emitted loud reports like pistol shots. Two bergs collided with a massive thump, grinding together with brittle, ringing booms for minutes after. There was a babble of excited conversation.

'Well, that certainly broke the ice!' Carol commented.

The exhausted berg I'd seen keel over on our first day out didn't really count. This was the first. Later we were to see bigger and even more spectacular capsizes, but the first one you never forget.

As always, we worked hard to get on the water that morning: taking down the tents, battling with sleeping bags to force the air out of them and stuff them into waterproof containers that they didn't really want to go into, carrying the gear down to the water's edge. Then the kayaks: ramming, pushing and punching to perform the daily miracle of making everything disappear inside our boats (well, nearly everything), and finally, sliding into the cockpit, stretching the spray deck over the combing, pulling on the paddle mitts – and away!

You might imagine that following a coastline would be a simple matter. Well, it isn't and it wasn't, particularly in a mist. There were confusing clusters of islands to be threaded through, icebergs that looked like islands, islands that merged with the mainland, and bits of the mainland that were easily mistaken for islands; channels with narrow entrances you could paddle past without seeing, and enticing gaps which looked like channels but instead were dead ends such as small fjords, bays or creeks. Did we ever get lost, or argue about where we were or point in several different directions at once? What do you think?

The Inuit might not have had compasses or satellite location finders, but they did have the benefit of years of close observation of their environment. Apart from watching the position of the sun in the sky, they might listen for the voices of seabirds in known colonies on the cliffs, or note the passage of migrating birds. Incidentally, my own experience of approaching the huge gannet colony on the Bass Rock in a mist is that you smell it before you hear it and you hear it before you see it. The Inuit were wise to the way snow ridges and ice crystals aligned themselves with the prevailing wind. They might look for the trend of cracks in the sea ice because these revealed the presence of capes and headlands still invisible in the distance. They also used 'sky maps'. A distant body of open water in the sea ice will often cast a dark shadow in the clouds above, while ice lying over the horizon will produce 'ice blink' (a soft white reflection in the air above it). Inuit travelling by kayak or sledge often carried navigation rods. These were pieces of bone along the edge of which were carved the outlines or silhouettes of each headland that would be passed between one place and another. I have heard it said that Inuit kayakers could locate their position in a mist by tasting the water. I suppose this is not as far-fetched as it sounds if one considers that the salinity would vary according to proximity to fresh water rivers and waterfalls entering the sea.

You might also imagine that sitting and paddling day after day, hour after hour, is a rather monotonous and boring occupation. Well, it isn't and it wasn't. In the first place, the sea is never the same from one day to the next and often not even from one hour to the next. Wave conditions vary enormously according to the strength and direction of the wind, according to whether the tide or current is moving in the same direction as the wind (long rolling waves) or in opposition to it (steep, choppy waves). Then again, the sea becomes distinctly lively if the waves are bouncing over shoals or meeting head-on other waves that are being thrown back from a cliff face. And at headlands and the ends of islands, where currents converge, the waves behave differently again, kicking up in all directions.

If the waves are not keeping you fully entertained, there are always your companions to talk to or your own thoughts to keep you company. I have read quite a number of books about the nature of creativity and several of them have said the same thing – that just about the best thing a writer can do is go for a walk. Physical activity and movement stimulates the brain, while the steady rhythm of walking releases the subconscious mind to wander at will, feeding off the slowly changing scenery. The same is true of paddling along at a steady pace in a kayak. I have had some wonderful daydreams, ideas and fantasies while out in my kayak.

Despite the mist, the icebergs seemed to radiate their own light, their brightness being emphasized by the sombre rocks and dark greens and browns of the dwarf, scrubby vegetation behind them. Occasionally this Precambrian landscape of polished, scoured and abraded rock would be dotted with huge boulders, a reminder that the glaciers, which had scraped the land bare, also deposited their load in places. I swung my blade, left, right, left right, taking pleasure in measuring this coastline, not against miles per hour in an engine powered boat, but in terms of human effort and muscle power, appreciating its true scale. I felt overawed by the insignificant span of human existence compared to the age of the rocks we were passing, formed when there was no life on earth. Stand with your arms held out to each side and let the extent of the Earth's history be represented by the distance between the tips of your fingers on your left hand and the tips of your fingers on your right hand. If someone were to run a file across the nail of your right middle finger, then the time that humans have been on earth would be erased.

'A penny for your thoughts, Bones,' Heather shouted across the gap between us.

'I was thinking how this Greenland scenery can humble you and elevate you at the same time.'

'Trust you to have peculiar thoughts like that!'

My bows dipped and lifted, shedding water, reminding me that the oceans were just as ancient as these rocks that filled me with awe. It did however raise the tricky question of how old is something that is continually renewed. I told Heather the story about the ship of Theseus that, over the years, had every part replaced until nothing of the original vessel remained. Was it still the same ship or not?

'Hmm,' said Heather. 'You could ask the same of the human body, of course. I'm still me though.'

'But there's a twist to the story, Heather. As the old ship gradually fell apart, the bits floated to an island where a man patiently collected the pieces and put them together until he had built a complete ship. Which of the two ships was the real ship?'

'For Heaven's sakes, Bones! Stop thinking about stuff like that and enjoy the scenery.'

When we rafted up for hot drinks from thermos flasks and a snack of nuts, raisins and chocolate, I told the others about the Greenland kayak championships and the rope exercises. This prompted mention of the Arctic Games in Canada where contests are held between far-flung Arctic villages. Mostly they seem to involve arcane and gymnastically improbable feats such as the One Foot Jump in which the contestant has to balance on one foot, then jump and kick with the same foot at a ball suspended about seven feet up.

Another event requires balancing the entire body on one hand while reaching for a piece of dangling fur with the other hand. And there's a tea-making contest, which is really a test of skill in getting a blaze going from nothing but twigs and firewood. The blanket toss, a primitive kind of trampolining, although not a competition, is traditionally performed at the games. It originated as a means of getting hunting scouts high off the ground to spot game on the horizon of the flat Barrens.

As our rafted kayaks drifted gently forward, we could feel the air becoming colder, for although we couldn't see them in the mist, this section of the fjord was choked with icebergs. Stopping long enough to give our muscles a rest, but starting again before we got chilled was always a bit of a problem. So, as stretching and flexing turned to rib thumping and arm rubbing, we eased the raft apart and resumed paddling. As we wound our way through an archipelago of turquoise, cobalt, pearl and emerald islands of ice, the air noticeably chilled. The muffled roar of capsizing bergs filtered through the mist. Occasionally a swell would roll through our ranks, rumour of the unseen event. Anything that looked at all unstable we hurried past or tried to give as wide a berth as possible — not easy in this crowded channel.

In a break of clearer water Joan and I converged. She told me about her malamut dog and how it travelled with her in her Canadian canoe.

'What's the difference between a malamut and a husky?' I asked.

She said that the Hudson Bay Company officials used to speak of Eskimos as 'Huskies'. A husky is, therefore, a term used for any kind of Eskimo dog where the Hudson Bay Company is, or was, strong. But when the gold rush reached the Bering Sea, the stampeders encountered the Malligmiut Eskimos, a word meaning 'the people of the place where the waves are high'. The dogs purchased from them were Malligmiut dogs.

A fierce squall hit us. We plugged into the freezing wind for about an hour. Occasionally a wave would sluice up the bow deck of a kayak, parting at the apex in front of the cockpit, foaming white, so that it looked as though the kayak had sprouted a pair of wings. Ahead, we spotted a bay and a sandy beach backed by a mist filled, snow streaked valley. A pale and feeble sun rested on the valley's left hand ridge. On the opposite ridge sat a waning moon.

'Early lunch!' Cathy shouted and nobody disagreed.

The beach was crowded with stranded icebergs, mostly little ones, as transparent as glass, and lying about at all angles. Beyond a line of dried seaweed of startling pink, a caribou's tracks ran the length of the sickle of sand. Standing on that beach, wet through and in the freezing wind, surrounded by ice, I was colder than I've ever been in my life. Carrying the kayaks out of reach of the advancing tide restored feeling to numb limbs. Then, while a valiant

The coldest beach

few struggled to create shelter in this shelter less landscape by erecting the tarp, the rest of us went for a run, leaping and bouncing around the barren moor till we glowed with the exertion.

Over mugs of hot soup we decided we were due half a rest day and that this was the place to pitch camp. A site without a steep haul between beach and hinterland was too good to pass up; besides, nobody relished paddling into the freezing wind, which had gained in strength since we landed. My journal for this day, written in an almost illegible hand because of cold, stiff fingers, comments: 'the kayaking is not particularly demanding, but Arctic conditions are'. Trying to relight the primus stove that had gone out, Valdemar burnt his hand. However, instant first aid was available. Valedmar simply stepped outside and pressed the injured part to a beached berg. The strong wind brought forth a new strategy for erecting the tents. Once the boulders had been collected, the tents were put up inside the tarp, then carried out and quickly anchored. 'I've never put up a tent inside a tent before,' Louis said.

My absence from the tent was required while Louis spring-cleaned its interior before undertaking his daily all-over wash, using his folding canvas basin and his allowance of hot water. As for me, I usually chose to make a pot of tea with my allowance.

'Don't forget to water the plants and dust the chintz curtains!' I called as I departed. 'No, Robin, I won't. And don't you forget to take your boots off when you come back in.'

I wandered amongst the ice sculptures on the beach, feeling the different surface textures: ribbed, honeycombed, pitted, frosted, or as smooth as only ice can be. I let my hands slide from one curving plane to the next, touching diamond edges, examining arches and holes, exploring shape, light and space in forms hitherto unborn, thrilled and delighted anew by each fresh angle. The abstract sculptor Barbara Hepworth has been described as someone who knew the mysteries of making space visible, as one who expressed a spiritual longing for the sublime. Had she stood on this Greenland shore she would surely have recognised a master sculptor greater even than herself.

Back in the pristine tent, a sweet smelling Louis and I stretched out on our sleeping bags. To a background of grumbling, growling bergs, punctuated by a distant crash or roar, we talked about French Canada. Ottawa, the Canadian capital, is divided in two by the Ottawa River. On the one bank you're in Ontario, on the other in French Canadian Quebec. Which explained what I couldn't fathom when I arrived: why one part of the city was having a public holiday while the other half wasn't. Louis, who lived and worked on the Quebec side, usually spoke nothing but French. To come on this trip he'd had to dust the cobwebs off his English. Occasionally, Louis, Marc and Guylaine would speak French together, but mostly, not wishing anyone to feel excluded, they conversed in English. 'I suppose it's our turn to help with the meal,' Louis said.

Joan and Cathy were in charge of the cooking, with the rest of us acting as helpers. There was no official rota, but everyone kept a kind of mental tally of when they were due to lend a hand again, either with the preparation or with the washing up. It seemed to work.

'If only we could sit round a good, blazing fire,' I said, pulling on my boots. 'It would make such a difference.'

But in Greenland there are no trees and so few people that there is no driftwood on the beaches, either from woodland or from the ubiquitous fish boxes, ships' timbers and other combustible jetsam such as is found on Scottish shores. Some of my fondest memories of kayak camping around the coast of Scotland are to do with the campfires that have kept us company in the evening. A good fire somehow encourages conversation and contemplation as you sit there feeding it, watching the stars, drying out bits of clothing held on the end of a stick and waiting for the foil wrapped potatoes to bake in the ashes. I described a trip I'd done out to the Summer Isles. It had poured with rain for the entire three days. Somehow we managed to get a fire going and then built it up till it gave out so much heat that we could stand beside it in the drenching rain and dry off faster than the rain could wet us.

An ice sculpture

We walked over the rough ground towards the tarp, noticing how its blues and whites harmonised with the ice in the bay. And so to another meal. The amount we ate never ceased to amaze me. There were days when merely standing on the beach doing nothing we must have been burning huge numbers of calories just to keep warm. We had at least three big meals a day, with biggish snacks in between. There were 14 bags labelled, 'Day One', 'Day Two' etc. Then there was the 'wanagin' bag, containing items in everyday use like butter, jam, salt and pepper. Then another with refills for staple items, and a spare bag and one with luxury items, treats and surprises. It didn't quite work. By day six we were eating day nine, partly because nobody could find day three. A simple question like, 'Is this day eight?' might receive the answer, 'Well, actually, it's day seven, but we're calling it day ten, unless, of course, you've found day three'.

No doubt we could have got by with less and we could have economised on space by carrying items that were less bulky, but also less tasty. In these latitudes, though, food is a very important factor in keeping up morale. It is not something to be skimped on.

All this is far removed from what the Greenland Inuit traditionally ate. They ate less fruit and vegetable than any other people on earth, yet scurvy and other vitamin deficiencies were rare. They ate some plants: the leaves of sorrel, the roots of vetch, seaweed, berries, and some which were obtained second-hand, so to speak, like the fermented contents of a caribou's stomach or partly digested willow buds from a ptarmigan's gizzard. The habit of eating raw meat is what supplies the Inuit with the vitamins they need for good health. *Muktuk*, the raw skin of the narwhal, contains as much vitamin C per unit weight as oranges, while raw seal liver is rich in vitamins A and D. In fact, the polar bear's liver contains so much vitamin A that it is poisonous. The sweetish, rubbery seal intestines, crammed with partly digested shrimps is another rich source of vitamins.

One of the main problems in Arctic survival, however, is not food, but water. In the far north the air is so cold it cannot hold moisture, which means that the body loses as much as a gallon of water a day through the nose and breathing passages as it automatically humidifies this very dry air. Dehydration can be a greater problem in the Arctic than it is in the Sahara, because when you are cold you don't feel as thirsty as when you are hot and therefore tend to drink less. You have to force yourself to take fluids. Since melting down snow and ice into drinking water uses up large amounts of precious fuel, avoiding dehydration is also often a question of fuel supply.

Our own menus were noticeably short on raw blubber or the kind of things one reads about in heroic tales of adventure, like pemmican, jerky and hard tack. Talking of the latter, my father used to recount how, as a boy in Anglesey, he would go down to the sands where the puffers were beached and beg a few ship's biscuits from the crew. They were large, round and exceedingly hard and fitted exactly into a porridge bowl. Softened with warm milk they made the perfect breakfast. Not like some ship's biscuits, it seems. It was fairly usual in the days of sailing ships to tap the biscuits on the table before eating them — it alerted the weevils that it was time to abandon biscuit. A standing joke concerning weevils was: 'Well, the cap'n promised us fresh meat every day, didn't he?' And there's an account of a voyage in the tropics where the maggots were so bad that the crew preferred to eat the mush made from the hard tack in the dark. One well-tried method of getting rid of the weevils and maggots was to open the canvas bag or barrel a week before its contents were due to be consumed and place a fish on top of it to lure them out. Each day the maggot-infested fish would be thrown overboard and replaced until the day came when the fish was found to be free of maggots.

Pasta was high on the list of things we ate and various dough mixtures that produced pancakes, flapjacks and pizzas. We carried pitta bread and a kind of rye bread that seemed to stay fresh forever, and a good selection of German sausage and salami-type meats that wouldn't go bad on us. We also had refried beans, powdered egg, cheese, vast quantities of peanut butter and jam, packet soups, rice and lots of other things in smaller quantities. Oh yes, and GORP, which stands for good old raisins and peanuts, consumed by the handful at every short break. To my surprise there was no porridge, considered as an absolute essential on any of our Scottish trips. Oatmeal porridge, brown sugar and evaporated milk come close to meeting that longing for the sublime. On weekend trips in Scotland tinned food plays a fairly major role. In order to save weight on the Greenland trip, however, we carried none.

Everyone brought a few personal treats and extras. In my case it was chocolate bars. In Heather's case it was one single herbal tea bag which she was confident would last the whole trip. Once or twice she would offer me a quick dip of it. Even after day two or three the difference it made to a mug of water was negligible.

As we ate our meal in the tarp we discussed the role that tinned food (canned to my Canadian friends) had played in both polar exploration and in naval warfare. By 1847 it was in common use in the navy, banishing the horrors of scurvy and of 'salt horse' (so called because unscrupulous victuallers would substitute horses from the knacker's yard for the beef they were contracted to supply). Even more important from the Admiralty's point of view was the fact that tinned food extended the period a ship could stay at sea without re-provisioning. The invention of bully beef profoundly influenced naval strategy.

Tinned food was also less easily got at by rats, although ships' rats, which could gnaw through wooden barrels and most other things, have been know to penetrate the cans. Elisha Kent Kane, the American Arctic explorer, once remarked, 'If I was asked what, after darkness, cold and scurvy, are the three besetting curses of our Arctic sojourn, I should say rats, rats, rats'. The Brown Norway rats, which thrived in polar darkness, could breed up to 13 times a year, producing litters of anything up to twenty at a time. You don't have to be a mathematician to see that, once infested, a ship could be overrun by rats. Vermin were not the only cause of spoilage and wastage of precious provisions on expeditions. Mildew and mould spoiled flour, biscuits, peas, meat – most things, in fact, if they were stored in cold, damp conditions. Spoilage often reduced a ship's company to starvation rations long before the amount of food taken on board should have warranted it.

'Maybe all those cans didn't do Franklin any good,' Joan said, referring to a recent theory that food poisoning, due to faulty canning, was what accounted for the fate of the Franklin expedition in its bid to find the North West Passage. It has been suggested that, while the tinned food was being properly cooked on board in the galleys of the *Erebus* and *Terror*, the toxins were rendered harmless. But once they abandoned ship and were cooking their food over inefficient stoves or eating it raw, the toxins in the faulty cans became lethal.

The talk came round to the subject of polar bears. They, Valdemar informed us, were a rarity in this area, having been over-hunted. I didn't know whether to be relieved or disappointed. On the east coast, Valdemar confirmed, polar bears can be a real threat. Since they hunt for seals on the pack ice, a kayaker encountered there tends to be regarded as prey. Over a distance of two or three hundred yards a polar bear runs faster than a man. Fortunately, they're very curious beasts. There's a story about a sailor being chased across the ice. Sensing the bear gaining on him the sailor throws down his jacket. The bear stops to investigate, then begins to overhaul the sailor once more. The terrified man discards his hat, with the same result, then his shirt, then his trousers, and so on, until he arrives at his ship, just ahead of his pursuer, but stark naked. When I had been working on my original plan to paddle on Greenland's east coast, I consulted a young kayaker from England, who had recently been there, about the bear problem.

'Oh, it didn't really worry me,' he said. 'I realised I didn't have to run faster than the bear ... just faster than one other person in my group!'

Of all the animals the Inuit traditionally hunted, the polar bear was the most prized. Native hunters considered Nanuk to be wise, powerful and 'almost a man'. These days the Inuit hunt polar bears with rifles, but they still use their dogs to follow the scent, slow down the bear and hold it at bay until it is shot. The meat is eaten and the fatty oil sucked from the bones. The fur is made into warm trousers, *nanus* for men, *kamiks* for women. To pay respect to Nanuk's soul, the hunter used to hang up the skin in an honoured place in the igloo for several days. If the bear was male, the hunter provided him with tools such as knives and bow-drills. If female, the bear was offered skin-scrapers and needles. It was believed that, if properly treated in this way, a bear would share the good news with other bears who would then be eager to be killed. Inuit hunters say that a polar bear will sometimes cover its black nose while lying in wait for a seal. A Canadian biologist has recently claimed that this is not true, a statement backed up by other scientists. I think the people more likely to be right are the ones who have been observing the bears for centuries, not just a handful of years, and whose lives depended on knowing the bears' every move and habit.

Polar bears, the largest living carnivores on earth, feed primarily on seals. When these are unavailable they scavenge on the carcasses of whales. On occasion they will kill reindeer, young walruses, small rodents and sea birds. Their main method of hunting seals is to wait at their breathing holes for them to surface, or, when the seals haul out on the ice in summer, a steady stalk before a sudden charge. Studies have shown that there are high levels of PCBs (Polychlorinated Biphenyl) in the blubber of polar bears. PCBs are used in many industrial and commercial applications throughout the world. Entering the oceans, trace amounts of PCBs eventually make their way to the Arctic, are gradually concentrated as they rise up the Arctic food chain until they are ingested by polar bears, which are at the top of the chain. Although the manufacture of PCBs is now banned, it may take years to eradicate them from the wildlife food chain. Their effect is to damage the bears' immune system and also to cause malformed organs and reproductive failure.

Polar bears can live 20 to 30 years, but only a small proportion live past 15 to 18 years. These averages may be decreasing since PCBs are not the only threat to the polar bear population: other forms of pollution, climate change, drilling, mining, fishing and hunting all impact on the bears. Kills increased substantially in the 1950s and 1960s when hunters began using snowmobiles, motorboats and airplanes. Public concern about these methods led to an international agreement in 1973 banning the use of aircraft or motorboats for polar bear hunts.

Mention of the bearskin *nanus* or trousers, led us to question Valdemar about what, traditionally, the Inuit wore under these outer garments. Well, it varied from place to place, he said, but fairly typically it might be a fox-skin shirt with an almost airtight hood. Underneath that might be a second shirt, this one made of bird skins, worn with the down next to the body. The skins

Inuit clothing

were chewed by the women until they were soft and then sewn together. The skins of more than 500 auks might be required to make such a garment. Inside sealskin boots, bird skin socks were often worn along with an insulating layer of dried grass. Similarly, sealskin mitts might be well wadded with straw.

I woke next morning with the light filtering bluey-green through the walls of the tent. Why couldn't they make tents a colour that gave the impression of sunshine and warmth? The answer is to do with minimum impact camping, of which *How to Shit in the Woods* was only one aspect. Using equipment that made minimum visual impact was also part of it.

'Goldilocks didn't exactly set a good example,' Cathy reminded me. 'Eating the bears' food and messing up their home like that.'

I had chosen to sleep in my damp paddling clothes.

'I think it worked. They're almost dry, Louis.'

'And your enthusiasm for this little jaunt, does that remain undampened?'

'It certainly does ... I think. Can't say the same for my sleeping bag. It's definitely on the soggy side of dampish.'

The definition of the word 'dry' is a comparative thing. When we got back to Nuuk, to central heating and proper drying-rooms, I found that what I'd been thinking of as dry was, by the new standards, exceedingly damp.

The single kayaks were the thoroughbreds of the fleet, compared to which the doubles were plodding carthorses. For this reason there was an amicably agreed switch of kayaks so that those who wanted to could have a turn in the singles. And so it was that I found myself sharing a double with Heather: an unlikely pairing in a way, the youngest and the oldest members of the group. The person in the stern has the foot pedals that operate the rudder and thus might be said to be the one in control of the craft. Heather, by virtue of her grand total of three summers in a kayak, compared to which a quarter century of experience was a mere nothing, claimed the stern position.

'And I'll be able to watch you and give you a few pointers.'

'So kind of you, Heather.'

Is that icebergs grinding, or my teeth? Ever hear about the young person who couldn't understand why her parents were so incredibly stupid and perverse throughout her teens, only to become really quite human and intelligent in her twenties? Clearly, a similar miracle had not occurred in my case.

We coped with our differences by exaggerating them and making them public property.

'Just my luck, Louis!' I shouted across the water. 'I've been stuck with the paddling partner from Hell!'

Greenland national dress

'And I've been stuck with a senile senior citizen from Scotland!' Heather broadcast to all and sundry.

We each invested the other with a fictional character. Heather, who was in fact, a nice, well brought up girl, became a hard drinking, hard swearing, harridan, who, on a scale of one to ten for marriage ability, scored minus five. This quickly turned into a kind of game with a ritual exchange of insults at the breakfast gathering, drawing the plaudits of the crowd. The day wasn't the same without it. Despite ourselves, we became firm friends.

'I've decided to award you a bonus ten Brownie points. Your score is now two.'

'So kind of you, Robin.'

And, to everyone's surprise, at the next chance of a change around, we agreed to stay together.

'After all, nobody else would have the patience to put up with you, Heather.'

'And nobody else would be willing to have a complete passenger in their kayak, Robin.'

What did Heather and I talk about all day? Well, we didn't quarrel all the time. I asked her about her flat and how it was furnished (eclectically ethnic); about her plans for the future (undecided); her boyfriends (disappointing); her opinion of French Canadians (not good); the many wilderness trips she had done (thanks to rich parents); the things Valdemar had said to her (did I sense a budding romance?); what would you do if you won a million dollars? (more travel, mostly); when did you last cry and why? (when I saw you for the first time); what was your scariest experience? (ditto). We discovered a common interest in photography of the kind that consists of seaweed, rocks and grained wood, with not a human face in sight. And a common admiration for the landscape photographers Ansel Adams and Edward Weston, who captured an unspoiled, unexploited America when it was still possible to believe in a heroic wild land and when there was no need to deliberately omit the pylons, the motorway, the parking lot and the litter.

I also asked her if she thought that, on this trip we were doing, there was an element of playing at being explorers and pioneers, rather like the 18th century courtiers who imagined they were returning to some simple rustic idyll by pretending to be poor shepherds and shepherdesses, dressed in their elegantly designed 'rags', until it was time to banquet in the evening.

'You know, you can spoil things by analysing them too much,' Heather replied. 'I bet you were one of those kids that took things to pieces and then couldn't put them together again.'

Our route for the day would take us through the narrow sound at the top end of the two islands of Qornoq (meaning narrow passage) and Qeqertarssuaq (which translates as Big Island). Here, we knew the ice would congregate, forcing us to pick our way carefully through it. The little island of Qornoq was the former site of another Viking farm. Qornoq illustrates much of the recent history of Greenland. In the 1950s, rather than try to provide modern medicine and education to the many scattered settlements, the government concentrated the population in a few towns and larger villages. The residents of Qornoq, about 80 in number, were offered favourable terms to resettle in Nuuk and almost the entire population of the island were housed in a high-rise block, Apartment Block 17. However, these former hunters and fishermen found town life not entirely to their liking and lobbied to be allowed to return to Qornoq.

In the spring of 1987 an unusually large run of cod came up the fjord and the villagers were given permission to return for the season, with the promise that, if the fishing could be sustained on an economic basis, they could return permanently. As far as I know, this didn't happen and the island is now a summer camp for children, a rendezvous for weekend parties and a stopping place for caribou hunters.

For me, though, Qornoq was, above all else, the birthplace of Manasse Mathaeussen who died in 1989, aged 74. Manasse was a legendry figure whose long career as a master kayaker has never been equalled. When he retired in 1986, he was still unsurpassed in skill. He was the only Greenlander who could perform all of the rolls, braces and rescue manoeuvres that Greenlanders have developed over many centuries. Manasse did more than any other person to keep interest in traditional kayaking alive, being the star performer at demonstrations even in his seventies. It was Manasse who taught Gino Watkins how to roll a kayak. The following are extracts from an account Manasse wrote of his life, about eight months before he died:

'My father moved to Ammassalik. He was appointed chief catechist (native teacher and minister) in Kulusuk where we stayed for 10 years.... this was the place where I learned how to paddle and roll in a *qajaq* and become a seal-catcher.... my whole existence as a seal-catcher consisted of training and then more training. Incorporated in this training was naturally how to handle animals that attack... Until my fiftieth year I could roll a *qajaq* no matter what equipment I used. Even the least bit of equipment I could use to get up ... I could pick up a stone from the bottom and use that to get up by... I have experienced sailing around without being able to see a seal. When I heard a ringing in my right ear I would stop and the seal would be there. When I dreamed about seals I was especially eager, because then I would catch not only one, but several.... What has pleased me most in my life as a seal-catcher is when I have been able to provide free food for the poor and the elderly, and those who did not have a seal-catcher in the family.... Today, in my seventy-second year I am starting to get pains in my back. It is of great importance for *qajaqing* to have a good back and to be flexible.'

There were no boats in the bay when we landed on Qornoq. We followed a narrow wooden railway line up to the cluster of wooden summerhouses. The rail was once used for the carts that carried the catch of fish up to the village, where they would be gutted, hung up to dry, or smoked. The deserted houses or chalets stood in a flowered meadow, rather like the meadows of the Monarch Isles west of Uist and Harris, unspoiled by chemical sprays and modern farming. Pooling our rather scanty knowledge of Arctic plant life, we identified, with no great degree of certainty, the Arctic poppy, dwarf fireweed, purple saxifrage and willow herb. It wasn't a day for lingering, though, and we were soon impatient to return to our snug kayaks and to recapture the bodily warmth that paddling bestows.

In tandem with Heather, I paddled into the mist on the stillest, most breathless day we had yet encountered. We glided across a liquid mirror, marvelling at the almost perfect reflections of ourselves and of the icebergs, sliding through emerald pools and lakes of deepest bluest blue imaginable. Moving in single file, we wound silently through the ranks of this frozen fleet. I remembered having read somewhere that some icebergs can be so near the brink of imbalance that even the vibrations of a ship will capsize them, while others explode if you so much as whistle. I found that, when I spoke to Heather, I was whispering. At times the mist thickened so that sea and sky and bergs merged until we floated in a dimension of our own through ambivalent, imperceptible qualities of white and grey, sliding through shoals of waxing suns, smooth swells gliding out of nowhere to unseen shores.

This merging of sea and sky put me in mind of whiteout conditions I'd met in the mountains. On one occasion in North Wales, the snow and the sky were completely indistinguishable. All around was a blank white sheet, no shadows, no near or far. The only way we could tell whether we were moving uphill or downhill was through the sensation in our legs. If we were on course, there

Paddling in the mist

ought to be a lake in a corrie somewhere below us.

'There it is!' I shouted.

I took a step forward, trod in a puddle and realised that this was my lake.

The Arctic explorer, Stefansson, once spent an hour stalking a tundra grizzly that turned out to be a marmot. Anthropologist Colin Turnbull in his book *The Forest People* gives a reverse example of this complete confusion of distance and scale. He took a group of pygmies in his Land Rover from the dense jungle to the open savannah. Because they'd lived all their lives enclosed by trees, they'd never seen anything more than a few feet away. So, when a herd of buffalo appeared in the distance, they thought it was a swarm of flies and were amazed and frightened at the way the flies grew bigger and bigger.

'Have you ever seen a Brocken Spectre, Heather?'

'What's that?'

'It's your own shadow magnified on low cloud, like the sun was the projector and the mist a big silver screen.'

Only the previous winter I'd seen the biggest and best I'd ever met. For half a mile, this 40-foot figure, framed by a circular rainbow, had accompanied me along a ridge, raising its ice axe in salute, when I raised mine. Valdemar paddled alongside.

'If only you could see the peaks. Just here they're really spectacular.'

Dramatic ice sculptures

Heather splashed him with her paddle. 'Why did you have to tell us that?'

Valdemar teased her by calling her names in Kalaallisut, the meaning of which she knew not. She appealed to me for help and soon returned to the fray, armed with some choice Scots phrases.

'Clartie wee midden!' she retaliated. 'Fushionless gomerell!'

We fell silent again, spellbound by the stillness of the scene. My son Glyn, who composes electronic music, recently brought out a CD entitled *Ocean of Serenity*. In a lecture I later gave, I used his music to accompany the slides I'd brought back of this misty, ice-girt passage, the eerie, disembodied sounds flooding the lecture hall like the pure essence of that day.

It was on a day such as this, on the Firth of Forth, drifting in our kayaks on a horizon-less mirror, that my late friend Mark had an apparently inexplicable bout of capsizing. Not a wave in sight, yet he simply could not stay upright. Only later, when I read a book called *Becoming Half Hidden: Shamanism and Initiation amongst the Inuit*, did I understand the reason. The author, Daniel Merkur, mentions a phenomenon known as 'kayak angst,' which was common amongst the Inuit. Hunters out in their kayaks, encountering these very still, hazy conditions, would fall into a trance, capsize and drown. Peter Freuchen, who lived, hunted and explored in Greenland for most of his life, describes

A Shamanic trance image

how, in the Greenland fjords where spells of completely quiet weather occur when 'there is not enough wind to blow out a match and the water is like a sheet of glass,' the kayak hunter must sit absolutely still in his boat so as not to scare the shy seals away. Even the slightest move might mean losing his prey. The glare of the sun, low in the sky, and the reflection from the mirror-like water hypnotizes him, so that he is unable to move and may remain in this trance until perhaps a slight ripple of wind on the surface of the water brings him back to reality.

In modern terms this would be classed as the result of sensory deprivation. Merkur cites kayak angst as an example of the readiness with which Inuit people fell into mild trance-like states. Led by their shamans, assisted by drumming and chanting, the Inuit of old habitually went into such states. The shamans themselves (or *angakoks* as the Inuit call them) went into much deeper trances to obtain the mystical faculty known as *qaumaneq*, the ability to 'see one's self as a skeleton'.

The blade of Heather's paddle poked me in the back.

'Hey, Bones! You're not paddling! Are you in a trance, or what?'

At the end of the trip, I asked each person which days stood out in his or her minds. There was little agreement, except for this one day that everyone remembered as something very special. We might have missed the spectacular peaks, but the mist provided its own mysterious beauty, its own aura of serenity.

Late in the evening we rounded the north end of Qeqertarssuaq and headed south down its eastern coast until we came to a smaller island about a quarter of a mile off shore, named Ummannaq, which means the shape of the heart. From sea level there was no knowing whether or not it lived up to its name, but the map confirmed that it was indeed heart-shaped.

Ummannaq Island was once the home of a community of hunters. The settlement had a church and, for a time, a team of German missionaries worked here. The missionaries had wind instruments and gave open-air concerts that are now said to have sounded nothing short of heavenly.

Our campsite on Ummannaq was half ringed by granite cliffs. Unstable icebergs crammed into the narrow channel between Qeqertarssuaq, and us whose snow-patched, torrent-streaked walls occasionally revealed themselves through the mist. In our sleeping bags, with the flap of the tent open to the soft grey light, we listened to the icebergs booming, thundering and crashing, the echoes reverberating round the cliffs.

'Sounds like the battle of the Titans,' I said.

'Or a Wagnerian concert,' Louis replied.

We talked of the Disko Bay glacier, further up the coast from us, one of the fastest moving in the world, travelling at 40 metres a day and producing a thousand icebergs a year — something in the order of 140 million tons of ice unloading into the sea. Before coming on the trip I tried to read up about ice. To my surprise, the computerised catalogue at Glasgow University indicated the library held no less than 95 books or papers on the subject. My joy was short-lived. ICE stood for Institute of Civil Engineering.

The parts of Coleridge's *Rime of the Ancient Mariner* that are set in the Antarctic, were, in fact, based upon accounts written by the early Arctic voyagers, John Davis, Frederick Martens and Dithmar Blefkins, all of whom had sailed up the west coast of Greenland and entered the Nuuk fjords. I read out the lines I'd copied into the back of my journal.

> *The ice was here, the ice was there,*
> *The ice was all around:*
> *It cracked and growled and roared and howled*
> *Like noises in a swound...................*
> *The ice did split with a thunder-fit:*
> *The helmsman steered us through!*

It was not difficult to believe that one of those ancient seamen, whose diaries Coleridge had read, had camped on this very spot and spent a night like this, listening to the ice. Incidentally, Coleridge, who was a regular smoker of opium and who wrote his celebrated poem, *Xanadu* while under its influence, knew about 'the Greenland wizards,' as he called them, and their use of the magic mushroom.

Next morning, unbelievably, the sun was shining. Above thin strips of cloud, as if disembodied, jagged grey-blue ridges, straight from Tolkien's imagination bit into a clear blue sky. In the sparkling water, the icebergs shone with diamond brilliance. It was a day for barrier cream, dark glasses and even a tentative discarding of an outer shell or two. Despite the gleaming, glinting beauty of the icebergs around us, my eyes lifted again and again to the peaks. It was our first real sight of them. At four to four and half thousand feet, they were not particularly high, but their dramatic towers, spires and thin pointing fingers commanded attention. A part of me was up there amongst the glistening snowfields, crunching across the hard crust on crampons, drinking the champagne air cupped in the high corries. Above the highest peak a white-tailed sea eagle soared. The sight of it released a silent song inside me and gave it wings.

'Steer to the left, Heather. I want to get a shot of the hills through that berg. The one close to the shore.'

'There's a better one further on... like a glass cathedral.'

White-tailed sea eagle

'Steer left.'

'No.'

'All right, have it your own way... as usual.'

Satisfied she had won her point, Heather steered left. Backlit by the sun, my berg glowed pink, cerulean, emerald, the colours amplified like those of a stained-glass window, but it never seemed to get any closer. Distances, I discovered, can be very deceptive in the clear Arctic atmosphere. What I thought was about a quarter of a mile away was more like two miles away. A 16th century sea captain, Mogens Heinson, had a similar experience. He was sent by Frederick the Second of Denmark to search for the lost Greenland colonies. Sighting tall cliffs, he set course for them. After several hours of sailing under full canvas he seemed no nearer than before. So powerful was this impression that he became convinced his ship was being held motionless over an underwater lodestone. Filled with fear, he put about and returned to Denmark.

We passed close to an iceberg about the size of a two-storey house. A big ledge of ice jutted out about three feet above the waterline.

Jokingly, I shouted to Cathy, 'Just paddle under that while I take a photo!'

To my astonishment, she did, flattening herself along the deck of her kayak to fit into the narrow space beneath the overhang. Heather talked about canoeing the lake and river systems of the Canadian Barrens. Listening to her, I began to understand the importance of watersheds, the higher ground you have to portage over to get from one river system to another.

'Look, caribou!'

Six of them stood silhouetted on a ridge above our nearest shore, all with curving, branched antlers. By one of those seeming coincidences that, I think,

Cathy doing a dare

are not coincidence at all, they were exactly framed by an eroded iceberg whose fretted shape mimicked the antlers.

There appears to be some disagreement as to whether the words caribou and reindeer are interchangeable or whether reindeer refers to the semi-domesticated North European variety of the species and caribou to the larger, wilder North American variety. The guidebook I bought in Nuuk refers to reindeer, but my Canadian companions called them caribou. South of where we were, on the Nuuk peninsula, the reindeer are semi-domesticated, being specially bred for their meat and rounded up each year for slaughter, but those on the ridge were wild and hunted as such.

The caribou is the only member of the deer family where the females also bear antlers. The human inhabitants of the Arctic have long depended on caribou for their meat, bone, oil, hides and sinews. The hair on their hide is hollow, giving it great insulating qualities, so that caribou hides are much prized for their warmth. Even today their sinews are preferred to modern thread for sewing leather garments since they have more elasticity and do not cut through the leather.

Caribou are both curious and short sighted. In the days before rifles were used, Eskimo hunters took advantage of this. Two men would walk past a herd, waving a piece of cloth to arouse the interest of their quarry. As they passed a boulder one would hide behind it and the other would continue on. The curious animals would follow him, past the man waiting behind the boulder. Another method of hunting them was to dig a pit and cover it with sheets of hard snow baited with dog urine that the caribou lick for its salt content. Caribou are also strongly attracted to human urine and it is not advisable to relieve yourself near a herd in case you are mobbed. It is known that caribou, like the Inuit shamans, will travel long distances for a chance to eat the magic mushroom. Whether this attraction to human urine is confined to the piss of those who have partaken of the mushroom or is more general because of the urine's salt content, I don't know.

In the Canadian Barrens where caribou have to swim across the lakes which form a greater surface area than the land, the Inuit hunted them from kayaks, the advantage of this being that a man in a kayak could move faster than a caribou could swim. On land, though, caribou are much faster. Only a few hours after birth a caribou calf can outrun a man. In the interior of Canada, without access to the resources of the sea, an Eskimo hunter used to have to kill at least 200 caribou annually to keep his family and his dogs alive and a tundra wolf must kill at least 16 caribou a year to survive. Those who observe caribou and reindeer herds at close quarters report on a noise like a thousand knitting needles click-clacking away. The animals click the tendons in their legs as a way of communicating, this being much more economical on heat and energy than grunting or bellowing.

As the caribou floated up the ridge, so near, yet so separate, I pondered on how little we really know about the wild animals of the Arctic. Researchers study only a tiny fraction of the whole population of any one species, for a small proportion of their lives, and even for that time are unlikely to be watching them constantly. Barry Lopez, in his book *Of Wolves and Men*, reckons that wolf research in Alaska amounts to about three one-thousandths of one per cent of wolf behaviour and that deductions made from such observations represent no more than good guesses. Heather talked about the herd from the Porcupine River of 60,000 caribou she'd seen migrating across the Canadian Barrens. She recounted how, in 1984, over 20,000 caribou drowned in the Caniapiscau River in Northern Quebec when Hydro-Quebec released water from a reservoir during the caribou migration. Somewhere in the middle of this I dropped off to sleep. Even in my sleep I kept paddling, but the slowing rate of stroke gave me away.

'Wake up Bones!'

'I deny everything!'

We stopped for a break on a small shingle beach. A dead, withered seal, lay above the tide-line with a bullet wound in its side. So slow is the rate of decay in the Arctic that it could have been there for several years. I felt as Brian Wilson did when, in kayaking round Scotland, he encountered a dead porpoise on a beach. In his book, *Blazing Paddles* he says of this experience that, 'Something had gone from the day and left a porpoise-shaped void'.

This was the first seal, dead or alive, I'd seen on the trip.

'Harp seals are the most common kind here,' Valdemar informed us. 'They keep away from the shore ... too many hunters. But they're out there in the middle all right.'

I said, 'I see more seals on my Scottish trips than I'm likely to see here. I didn't think it was going to be like that'.

I told him about the seals I'd met on my trip to the Monach Isles, west of North Uist. Each bay had its own colony that swam out to greet me and escort me to the boundaries of their territory. In his turn, Valdemar told me the legend of Neqivik, an orphan girl whom nobody cared for. When the settlement moved, the men tied their kayaks together into one big raft and loaded their families and all their belongings onto it. Neqivik they left behind. She swam after them, grasped the raft and tried to climb aboard, but they chopped her fingers off. Her chopped fingers became seals and walruses and other animals. She herself sank to the bottom of the sea from whence she rules all the animals of both sea and land. If people have obeyed all the taboos she sends an animal out to them, but if a taboo has been broken, she keeps the animals confined in her underwater house. Then an *angakok* or shaman must visit her and comb her hair — a task she cannot perform for herself because she has no fingers.

Launching again, we paddled for another three hours under blue skies and bright sunshine, enjoying the long clear vistas down the fjord and the shimmering flocks of ice. A flotilla of eider duck watched us paddle by. We landed again, followed by the usual hefting of kayaks up the slope and the search for boulders. It was routine by now. My diary for that day records: 'Got out dry (well, dampish) for the first time this trip.' It was too late in the day, though, to entertain any hopes that the low-lying sun would reduce the size of my bag marked 'wet.'

Later, Heather put her head through the tent in which Louis and I reclined. She surveyed my half of the space with a critical eye.

'Is this a demonstration of Chaos Theory, or what? And I think you ought to know, Louis, Robin's getting senile! He fell asleep in the kayak!'

'It's not the first time I've done it,' I said.

'Done what?' Heather wanted to know.

'Fallen asleep in a kayak ... except, the other time, I was in a single.'

I told them about the time, returning in the dark from a long, long day,

I had dozed off and capsized and woken up underwater and upside-down. The roll up again was pure instinct. And then I recalled the time I had fallen asleep during the Arctic Sea Kayak Marathon in Norway. This is a race round the Vesteralen Isles, the northern-most group of the Lofoten Isles, which takes place over five days. 'Race' is perhaps rather a flattering word. There were the serious racers, people (all men) of Olympic athlete standard, and then there were the ramblers — those who simply wanted to take part and complete the course. I was very definitely of the latter persuasion. There were well over 50 men and women ramblers: Scandinavians of all sorts, several from the various Baltic States, British, Dutch, German, all conversing with each other in impeccable English. I hadn't known until then how popular sea kayaking was in these countries, especially Sweden. Or what a variety of equipment and kayaks there were which are not normally seen in the UK. Some of the Russian designed kayaks were enormous. Out of them would emerge tents of the kind you can stand up in, folding tables, camp beds...

'Yeah, yeah, Bones, all very interesting, but what about the bit where you fell asleep?'

'Well, there was this one day when the route from one camp site to the next was about 40 miles with almost nowhere to stop on the way. In about the sixth or seventh hour of paddling I fell asleep. Only for a minute or two, I think.'

'How does Arctic Norway compare to this?' Louis asked.

Very different, I told him. The warm Gulf Stream current moves north up the coast of Norway. This and the absence of anything like Greenland's huge ice cap make the climate much milder. Arctic Norway is greener, with plenty of trees and other vegetation and fairly well populated. Almost every fjord had at least one small fishing village and we never paddled for long without a dwelling-place of some sort in sight.

'Maybe that was how southern Greenland was in the Middle Ages,' Louis commented.

'I remember Vesteralen's impressive jagged ridges and sharp peaks. Not as spectacular as here, though.'

Louis said, 'I can't believe I'll ever see anything to rival this.'

And Heather and I agreed with him.

When Heather had departed, I said, 'I think I'll do my meditation now.'

'Will I disturb you if I stay and write my diary?' Louis asked.

'No: as long as you don't address me directly. The odd shuffle or cough doesn't intrude.'

I sat with my back propped against a pile of waterproof bags. A blast of hail drummed on the fabric overhead. Several weeks before coming to Greenland I had been given an audiotape, the sounds of nature set to classical music 'for relaxation and meditation' – ocean surf, rain, thunderstorm, flowing water, the call of whales. They were all here: the mountain stream in the gorge to my left, waves breaking against the cliffs a hundred feet below me, the decreasing patter of the hail, and, perhaps not a thunderstorm, but the grumbling, rumbling bergs instead. And the whales were out there somewhere. Maybe, at a subliminal level, their signals were reaching me. In Buddhist paintings lamas and holy men are sometimes depicted carrying a bell that represents the perfect sound of voiceless wisdom. These sounds, which now whispered to my senses, contained that kind of wisdom.

But the Beholder Wanting

Could it be only nine days since we launched our kayaks at Nuuk? When the hours are crammed with new and intense experiences, the days assume Tardis-like dimensions, expanding for those who live inside them. We paddled in brilliant sunshine. It was a day that called for dark glasses and plenty of barrier cream to protect our faces not only from the sun, but also from its reflection off the ice and water. Our sheltered bay seduced us into divesting a windproof layer and maybe a sweater or two, only to regret it once we were past the headland and exposed to the chill wind. We were now heading southeast towards the entrance to Kapisigdlit Fjord. In every direction we looked bare flanked mountains rose steep and purple out of the sea, sweeping upwards to majestic corries packed with snow and sharp peaks trailing banners of morning cloud.

While I was in Ottawa, waiting to meet up with my fellow paddlers, I went to an exhibition of paintings by the Canadian artist, Lawren Harris whose main landscape period was from 1918–1930. It was through his eyes that I was now seeing the mountains around me. He was one of the Group of Seven who set out to find a style of painting which was uniquely Canadian and which would express the spirit of their land, the power of the landscape and the vastness of the North. Lawren Harris helped me look at the Greenland landscape with fresh eyes and appreciate its remote and monumental silence, its deep space, the beauty to be found in its minimalist elements of water, ice, rock, cloud and fog. He showed me the underlying geometry of the mountains, their simple, essential lines and curves and ephemeral cloudscapes on broad-winged breezes in perpetual harmony with the white-robed land.

As we entered the mouth of Kapisigdlit Fjord, the wind strengthened, as often happens when the same volume of air has to funnel down a more confined channel. It was at our backs, pushing us along, making paddling pleasantly effortless. We were hugging the north shore of the fjord. Some people like to be out in the middle, enjoying the space and freedom and the feeling of having cut all ties with the solid world. I prefer to follow a coastline within a yard or two, where it's easier to believe you're making progress when you can see the nearby objects passing by, and the eye can feast on the details of the rocks, their bands and strata, the lichens that pattern them and the myriad tiny shellfish which stud them. On this trip we were following a circular course and therefore not retracing our route. It never ceases to amaze me, though, how very different the same bit of coastline can be on the outward and on the return journey because one is seeing it at different states of the tide. In the morning, the sea might be thundering into caves, slapping against cliffs, and sluicing in and out of skerries; and in the afternoon, those same caves hang dark and silent ten feet above one's head, acres of shining seaweed and inter-tidal marine life are exposed, and what

The ice V

Morning clouds hang over sparkling ice

were small rocky islands are now the miniature peaks of a newly created world.

The glitter and sparkle of the icebergs was sheer delight. Fleets of them thrilled the eye. Displays of brittle crystal glass gave way to green dragons unfolding wings of jade, and flashing scimitars dissecting the great blue dream that was the sky. I remember a giant white V rising straight from the sea whose perfect reflection vanished in a fish splash. Tom and Carol in one of the red doubles closed within talking distance.

'What do you think of it so far?' I asked.

'Fantastic!' Tom answered. 'Not many places live up to the hype and expectations, but this sure does! This is everything I came for!'

I agreed with him. I had thought I would never see anything as magnificent or as breathtaking as the Grand Canyon in Arizona, but the Greenland icebergs were its match.

Louis, in a yellow single, drew level with us. 'When we land, Robin, could I persuade you to show me how to roll a kayak? We've both got wet suits we can put on.'

'No way, Louis! A heated swimming pool is the place to learn. Anyone who voluntarily capsizes here needs his head examined!'

Heather's voice came from the cockpit behind me. 'That would be difficult if it was underwater!'

Actually, although both the spirit and the flesh cringed at the thought of an encounter with the icy waters of the fjord, I have to say that anyone who believes they can roll a kayak on the strength of being able to do it in a warm swimming pool is misguided. It is not the same thing at all as being able to do it when you're unprepared for it, in a rough sea, with the shock of hitting the cold water robbing you of your senses.

The kind of reply I gave to Louis might well have earned me a Big Girl's Blouse Award had I been out with my regular paddling companions in Scotland. This award went, at the end of each trip, to the person who had most blatantly failed to live up to our tongue-in-cheek standards of being a macho man's man. Over the years, the award had been made for whimpering louder than anyone else when pulling on cold wet clothes (me), being caught with a bar of scented soap, being the last to express extreme disappointment that there was no time to tackle the horrendously rough passage round a headland (me again), and knowing how to operate the washing machine in the Galway cottage we had rented for the week (definitely not me).

And then we were nearly within striking distance of Kapisigdlit, a little fishing village at the head of Kapisigdlit Fjord.

I said, 'I think it's going to be the only permanent habitation we pass in a hundred and fifty miles or so of coast'.

Heather seized a chance to correct me. 'Wrong! We've passed a couple of small places in the mist.'

'Actually, I think I am wrong,' I agreed, 'Wrong about it being nearly 150 miles of coast. It depends on the scale you're using when you measure it'.

At a certain scale of map only the major indentations round the coast would be charted and measured. Increase the scale and smaller indentions within the larger ones begin to show up, adding to the measurable length of the coastline, and so on down to immense magnifications where the minute capes and bays have even smaller capes and bays within them, so that the coast begins to stretch to infinity.

'Yeah, I sometimes get that feeling when you're talking,' Heather remarked.

'I was interested in what you were saying the other day about the explorer, Charles Frances Hall,' Carol tactfully intervened.

We marvelled at the toughness and fortitude of the earlier explorers.

'Here we are, measuring our hardships in hours and days, but those guys, in far more extreme conditions, often over-wintering, endured deprivations and sufferings and separation that lasted for months and often years.'

'It's certainly given me a new respect for those guys,' Tom said.

Accompanied by slowly unfolding amazements of towering rock and glinting ice, I told them how Hall had recorded in his diary that the Inuit he met believed the earth had once been covered in water. On asking them why they believed this, the answer came, 'Did you never see little stones, like clams and such things as live in the sea, way up in the mountains?' — a comment that was made before European geologists were citing similar evidence for the marine origins of some of our present-day mountains. The Flood story, I said, was by no means confined to the Old Testament. It is a universal story, being found in the myths of many tribes and societies throughout the world. It was a bit ironic, I said, that in this day and age when we are doing our best to avoid worldwide annihilation, God's vengeful act of drowning the entire population of the world except for Noah and his family and a handful of animals, has become a cute little story for children, and a subject for primary school projects.

Heather's voice broke into my tirade. 'Hey, Bones! You're paddling like fury! Slow down!'

At that point we were passing a small rocky island about a quarter of a mile from the mainland. Behind its cliffs a steep conical mountain reared up. We rafted together for a handful of GORP and a bit of chocolate. While we rested, Valdemar told us the legend attached to this place. An Eskimo and a Viking had once held a contest to see who could shoot an arrow onto the island. The loser had to climb the mountain and jump off. In Valdemar's version it was the Eskimo's arrow that reached the island and the Viking who had to cast himself from the summit.

'I bet the Vikings tell it differently,' I said.

Heather flipped a scoop of water in Valdemar's direction. 'The Eskimo probably made sure he didn't have to jump by aiming his arrow at the Viking instead of the island!'

It was time to make a decision. Either we could paddle another two hours and camp before we got to Kapisigdlit (some guidebooks spell it Kapisillit), or we could aim to get there tonight, in which case we had another five hours of paddling on top of the five we'd already done. If we decided on the second plan we'd feel justified in taking a rest day tomorrow and it would give us time to climb a mountain where there were views of the icecap and the glacier.

Louis' eyebrows shot skywards. 'Climb a mountain? That's a rest day?'

'You know what they say,' Joan laughed. 'A change is as good as a rest.'

An anonymous voice was heard to mutter, 'Yeah, a change of underpants. I could certainly do with a change of underpants.' Which led Marc to recount the answer an explorer gave to a journalist on returning from a long expedition. When asked how often he had changed his undergarments, he replied, 'Once a month – John changed with me and I changed with him'.

I'm not sure whether it was the thought of a break from the paddling, or the lure of the icecap, or the chance to wash and dry a few clothes, but we all voted for Plan Two. While we had been deciding what to do, Kapisigdlit's monthly supply-boat, a small cargo ship, ploughed down the fjord, having delivered most of the necessities of life to the isolated community. The best part of the shopping is done by mail order catalogue, delivered once a month during the summer. For some northerly communities the supply-boat used to be an annual affair. In Inuktitut, the word used for 'catalogue' translates literally as 'the wishing book'.

Valdemar's story of the contest between the Viking and the Eskimo set me on a train of thought, which took me down the fjord another mile or two, about invisible and spiritual landscapes. The most important aspects of some physical features to a local community may be the stories and myths they evoke, their role as religious sites and as re-enforcers of the community's values, its sense of identity, its roots in the past, its relationships with the ancestors and the gods. I thought about the map of the Nuuk Fjords I had been consulting that morning and how, if an Inuit hunter had carried a map of the area in his mind it would probably have been quite different. The places noted and named would be where berries could be picked, the best cliffs for birds' eggs, regular haunts of polar bears. Possibly the spatial proportions of the hunter's map might have been based on the time it took to travel over that section of terrain (which would vary according to the season), and how important that place was or how much time was spent there.

'You've gone quiet, Bones.'

'You know how it is, Heather, the brain was browsing, the mind meandering.'

The wind grew brisk and blew us down the fjord on big rolling waves, reducing the estimated five hours to something nearer three. Kapisigdlit Fjord was an offshoot of the main artery down which the bergs floated, with the result that its upper end was free of ice. Slowly the little squares dotted along the shore and up the hillside grew bigger and became recognisable as houses in a variety of bright colours. Like the ones at Nuuk, they were wooden, prefabricated and shipped in from Denmark. One of them looked as though it should be the schoolhouse. A friend who had taught in Alaska told me that she'd soon learned that western admonitions like 'work first and play later' or 'always be punctual' were foreign, outlandish ideas to her students. Which brought to mind the training course I once conducted for teachers in South Uist. It was scheduled to start at 9 am and end at 3 pm. At quarter to ten the first participants straggled in and then, at two o'clock in the afternoon, several teachers wandered out, saying they had things to attend to on their crofts, but all done with such charm it was impossible to take offence.

'And that must be the church,' I said, pointing to the wooden spire close to a large oil storage tank.

The Inuktitut word *imaaqa*, meaning 'maybe', is, as I mentioned before, the most used word in the language. And, in similar vein, Inuktitut does not differentiate between 'if' and 'when'. With some frustration missionaries realised that their oft used phrase 'when Jesus comes' could be taken to mean 'if Jesus comes'.

There was a possible campsite at the very head of the fjord, about two miles past Kapisigdlit. Because it was late and we were tired and hungry and anxious to put the tents up before the wind got any stronger, we decided not to stop at the village but to press on down the fjord. Women and children came running out of the houses and onto the shore to wave and call out greetings. One well-endowed young woman called out what I think was more than greetings whilst flaunting her natural assets at us. Whether the men of the village were all out fishing in their motorboats, or they disapproved of our western-style kayaks, or they considered it undignified to stare at us I don't know, but only the women and children watched us pass by.

The waving, shouting villagers reminded me of Commander Clarke, who sailed round the world in his yacht sometime in the 1950s. He told me (and also wrote about it in a book called *On the Wind of a Dream*) that early in the voyage, having quarrelled with his companion, he hired a young West Indian to assist him. Somewhere in the Pacific they were approaching an island when boatloads of the local inhabitants paddled out to meet them, singing and cheering. They put garlands round the black youth and carried him off in a specially prepared craft, treating him as if he were some kind of deity. The islanders, it transpired, were followers of one of the many cargo cults prevalent in that part of the Pacific.

'What's a cargo cult?' Heather asked.

'A belief that, one day, all the goods and luxuries of the Western world will be delivered to them as a gift from the gods.'

Colonial administrations, I told Heather, had tried to stamp out these cults because people who were convinced they were about to be showered with all these goodies saw no need to work, to cultivate their fields or go out fishing. Consequently an upsurge of cargo cult prophecies was often followed by famine.

'Anyway, this particular cult had prophesied that the 'cargo' would arrive in a ship with white sails and with a black man at the helm.'

'Bet they were disappointed.'

'They seemed to get over it. Saw it as a kind of sign, a forerunner of better things to come.'

Heather said, 'Perhaps we should tell Marc and Guylaine to land here. They're the nearest we've got to a boat stuffed with all the luxuries of the West'.

I said, 'Quite a lot of expeditions break up because of bitter quarrels, so I'm told.'

'Yeah, I'm not surprised, Robin. Some people can be very irritating.'

'So they can, Heather.'

In the past, accounts of expeditions never admitted to any un-gentlemanly disharmonies occurring, preferring to present a rather more romantic view of their exploits than do modern adventurers who tend to be much more open about what really goes on. When confined together for a long period, in arduous and stressful conditions, companions can become intensely irritating to the point of hating them. Harmless mannerisms and habits assume the proportions of major flaws and deliberate attempts to annoy. One can build up a massive resentment against a person because of the way he drinks his soup, or because of some silly catch phrase he keeps using. If rations are short, it can seem that one's companion has secured the larger portion of a meal, and he invariably occupies more than his share of the tent.

Cracks of this sort had not, as far as I was aware, developed in our own group. Our little trip, of course, was nothing like as demanding as the serious expeditions that might produce the sort of strained relationships I have described. There were minor grumbles, but nothing more than that. Humour, patience, good manners, maturity and a willingness to fit into a team were evident in abundance and with these qualities came a remarkably harmonious group. A factor assisting this was that we were seldom confined together at close quarters. During the day we were often scattered over a fairly large area of water, the groupings of who was paddling alongside whom constantly changing. Similarly, on land the tents were, by necessity, pitched far apart, wherever a rare bit of flat ground presented itself. This is the reason why some of the people in our group are hardly mentioned in my account of this trip. Chuck, for example, always pitched his tent high up and the furthest away from the tarp, our social centre. He always paddled way out on the periphery of the fleet, and when we landed for a break he, being the intrepid biped with a tripod that he was, headed off with camera and equipment to some vantage point in search of a good shot. The smoke rising from Chuck's pipe as he paddled along was like a message that all was well with the world, but Chuck himself I hardly spoke to.

Ever since studying social anthropology at Cambridge I have been interested in the dynamics of small groups. We behave differently in groups from the way we do as individuals. Since we spend a large part of our time in one type of group or another, Socrates' advice, 'Know thyself,' might have been more appropriate in the plural: 'Know ourselves.' The way we behave in all-male groups differs from our behaviour in mixed groups. Furthermore, the influence of the group increases the more closed to outside influences it becomes. It was with great interest therefore that I kept an eye open for such facets of small group behaviour as the patterns of interpersonal relationships which developed; the degree of conformity within the group and how deviators were treated; the influence on personal attitudes and values of group norms; the way the group solved problems and made decisions; the roles which different members of the group assumed (leader, loner, jester, scapegoat); the development of a group humour, of in-jokes and an in-language; the causes of tensions within the group and the sorts of safety valves and releases which the group arrived at; the development of cliques, hierarchies and pecking orders and the unofficial power structure. All that, I suppose, is the subject for a different book than this, one that I shall probably never write.

We paddled on, past the big wooden shed with its open ends, where the split fish were hung on racks to dry in the wind. Then a final weary mile to a sandy beach, a stream flowing into the fjord and, oh joy, flat ground level with the beach where, the wind having died away to nothing, the bugs were out in force. Ah well, you can't have everything. A low carpet of what looked like dwarf bog myrtle provided a springy floor to the tent. Louis and I erected it with well-practised efficiency, for once using tent pegs instead of having to tie the guy ropes to boulders.

Inside the tent, Louis, who was writing up his diary, paused pencil in hand.

'Did we see any birds today?'

'I don't remember any.'

'Well, according to this book, northern diver, razorbill, gyrfalcon and white-tailed eagle can all be seen around here.'

'Not by me.'

'Me neither.'

In fact, we had seen very little of the wildlife since starting out. A silent kayak, free of engine noises and fumes, and with a shape suggestive of some sort of sea animal (especially when seen from underwater) and flipper-like means of propulsion, is an ideal craft for getting close to marine life. But, in a vast wilderness, I suppose it is a matter of luck whether one is in the right place at the right time. Had this been a bird watching or a whale watching trip, obviously we would have made a point of being in the right place at the right time, but doing a round trip and following a different agenda, we simply had not been lucky with close encounters of the chancy kind. I think one sometimes gets a false impression about the density and visibility of wild animals from nature films in which months, even years, of patient waiting are condensed into one hour. Tom passed by the tent, fishing rod in hand.

'I'm going to one of the small lakes higher up. Did you know that Kapisigdlit translates as salmon?'

Apparently, this is the only river in Greenland in which salmon swim upstream to spawn. Later Tom returned triumphant, not with a salmon, but with an Arctic char, which he generously donated towards the following day's breakfast.

In the tent that night, after a satisfying dried fruit curry (apricots, raisins, dates, cashew nuts, brown rice and chopped onions, served with chapattis), I relented a little and gave Louis the rudimentary theory of rolling a kayak. A kayak is controlled from the hips ('You don't sit in a kayak, you wear it,' is a favourite saying of instructors). When you are upside down, you perform a stroke with your paddle that gives you sufficient support from the blade to revolve your hips so as to bring the kayak upright. This stroke is a sweep from the bows towards the stern with the leading edge of the blade angled upwards so as to keep it on the surface. As the sweep comes to an end, and the kayak is halfway righted, you push the flat of the blade directly downwards, in effect pushing yourself upright.

'So there you go, Louis.'

'Mmmm,' said Louis doubtfully.

I was fully confident that my explanation was guaranteed one hundred per cent to result in a failed roll. It isn't quite as simple as I'd made out, and a lot of practice and preliminary drills are needed. One of the main problems is that, when you find yourself upside down in the water, it is all too easy to become disorientated. Everything that was on your right is suddenly on your left. What a moment ago was up is now down, and in murky water it is easy to lose a sense of where the surface is.

I lay in my sleeping bag listening to Louis thrashing about performing imaginary rolls. Outside the tent a rosy glow pervaded the sky. Although I couldn't see the mountains, I felt their presence. All that day, whatever we were doing, even when not looking at them, we had been aware of them, bringing to us a sense of both excitement and serenity, a new sense of proportion and humility as their vastness and timelessness sunk deep into our subconscious minds. Louis was breathing deeply and regularly now. To leave the warmth of my sleeping bag and exit the tent would mean the usual gymnastics of dressing in a confined space, pulling on my boots and braving the biting air outside. I was crazy to even be thinking about it.

I walked a little way up the slope and sat in the springy scrub. A light breeze had sprung up again: just the right amount to keep the mosquitoes and other bugs at bay. Clouds like slowly drifting windflowers bloomed in shades of pink. To the east the higher snow slopes blushed at the touch of the low lying sun and steep rock faces glowed like molten lava as though, any moment, they would pour in rivers of scarlet and gold into a sea bejewelled with floating rubies.

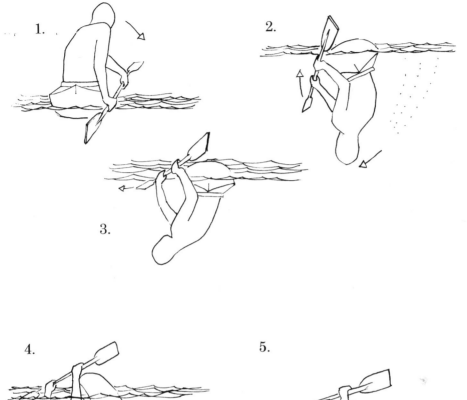

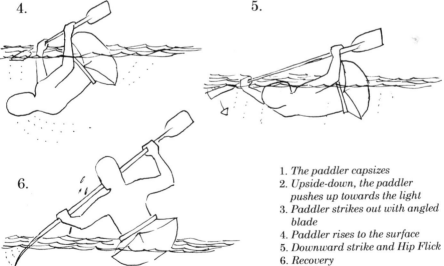

1. *The paddler capsizes*
2. *Upside-down, the paddler pushes up towards the light*
3. *Paddler strikes out with angled blade*
4. *Paddler rises to the surface*
5. *Downward strike and Hip Flick*
6. *Recovery*

Kayak rolling technique – The Screw Roll

Next morning, the start of our promised rest day, the sun was shining again. This was our first real chance to dry our clothes. Usually, when the sun was at its highest, we were paddling. Clotheslines slung from tent to tent or between tripods of paddles fluttered with multi-coloured garments. On the slopes behind this carnival scene three caribou grazed, apparently untroubled by our presence. We discussed what we were going to do with our free day. Several decided to paddle to the village, some to walk to the foot of the glacier, which was on the other side of a ridge, others to climb the peak which afforded a view of the icecap, and a few simply wanted to loaf about the camp doing nothing in particular.

Valdemar, Cathy, Marc, Guylaine, Tom, Carol and myself made up the party which was going for the 3,000 foot summit of Nivko whose lower flanks were directly behind our tents. Cathy, who had climbed it before, described it as rough terrain with the occasional snowfield, about an eight-hour day. Only minutes into the walk we lost the benefit of the light sea breeze. With cries of joy the bugs descended on us. Our dilemma was whether to remain covered up, sweating profusely as we toiled uphill with rucksacks on our backs, or to strip off and be eaten alive. I can well understand why travellers have said they suffered more from heat in the Arctic than anywhere else. I tried a compromise, removing the windproof layer but retaining the long-sleeved thermal vest. It didn't work. I could almost hear the scornful laughter of the bugs as they penetrated the vest's soft fabric. By the end of the day my body was a horrible mass of itching lumps.

'And the big lumps have smaller lumps and so on *ad infinitum*,' I told Heather later.

'This isn't going to be another of those boring lectures about coastlines and infinity is it?' she wanted to know.

The way alternated between low, dense scrub and sloping slabs of ancient grained rock. A noticeable difference between this and a Scottish hill was the absence of any footpaths. The 'easy' way up almost any Scottish hill has been trodden by thousands of feet. In the Alps some of the popular routes have large red arrows painted on the rock, pointing the way, and iron rungs hammered in to help you over the difficult bits. But here you could still get the feeling that you were actually picking your own route. I cursed my bug hat, feeling claustrophobic inside it as I struggled for breath. I cursed the way the fine netting diffused the strong sunlight so that I couldn't clearly see where I was placing my feet. And when those things seemed too much to bear and I removed the damnable thing, I cursed the bugs even more, remembering that a naked man in the summer in Greenland is likely to suffer approximately 9,000 bites per minute and lose half his blood in less than two hours. Well, I wasn't about to volunteer to test the truth of this statistic. 'Mosquitoes are friends that we find in Greenland,' said one of my guidebooks. Huh! Is what I say to that! 'The best way of dealing with them is not to let them 'bug' you,' the stupid guidebook continued. Double huh!

As we gained height the views opened out: silvery vistas down the fjords, their formations and relationships now discernible as on the map, ranks of snow-capped peaks to the north, the ice-choked upper reaches of Kangersuneq Fjord, into which the Kangersuneq glacier calved, gradually appearing over Nivko's shoulder. I was ahead of the others as I traversed a snowfield, my footsteps making the first marks on the sparkling, pristine expanse. Or so I thought, until they crossed a fox's tracks. On the edge of the snowfield dry reeds had described wide arcs in the snow where they had bent to yesterday's wind. Maybe it wasn't likely on this particular route to the summit, but there must still be many places in Greenland where no human has ever trod. I have even had that thought in some of the remoter parts of Scotland and wondered if my footprint was the first to be made there since time began. I pondered on the age-old dilemma of explorers. By exploring the wilderness that they love, do they sow the seeds of its destruction? By seeking out an unspoiled place like Greenland, were we helping to spoil it? By writing about it would I hasten this process? My reasoning, or my justification, was that the pleasure and spiritual renewal to be found there should not be some kind of secret known only to an elitist few, that everyone had a right to enjoy what I was enjoying, that informed opinion about the wilderness was better than ignorance, and anything that might help foster love and respect for the natural environment and might possibly contribute to its preservation was okay.

Finally we attained the summit and a welcome breeze. A rocky plateau was dotted with little wind-shivered lakes, or sheltered pools that reflected cauliflower clouds. In a high corrie on the other side of the glacier, jet-black ravens floated in a crystal bowl of Alpine air. Directly south of us, bordered by fjords, glaciers and the luxuriant Austmannadal Valley, was the area which is reckoned to be some of the best and most beautiful trekking country in West Greenland, with mountain peaks of 900–1,200 metres, intersected by wide valleys and strewn with lakes.

'Nivko means dried meat,' Valdemar told us.

'It's what we've become by the time you get to the top,' Carol replied, bottle of juice in hand.

We walked to the plateau's northern rim and sat on the edge of a sheer drop of 2,500 feet to Kangersuneq glacier. To the west the glacier merged into the fjord in a jumble of vast ice blocks that gradually separated out over a stretch of two or three miles and floated away as icebergs. To the east and to the north the icecap stretched flat and white to the horizon, a sepulchre for buried, age-old winters. Here the ice age continues unabated. The emptiness of it, the silence of it was impressive.

As we ate our packed lunches and refilled our dehydrated bodies, Valdemar told us that the icecap is almost 14 times the size of England and that, in its middle part, it is 11,000 feet thick. The weight of it has bent the rocks downwards to such an extent that the centre of Greenland is nearly 2,000 feet below sea level. Something like ten per cent of the world's fresh water is held frozen here. If it melted, the seas around the globe would rise by nearly 20 feet. The bad news is that, since 1978, polar orbiting satellites monitoring Arctic sea ice have observed a decrease in the ice's extent amounting to almost three per cent every decade. In the year 2000, scientists aboard a Russian icebreaker discovered an ice-free patch of water a mile wide at the North Pole – the first time the North Pole has turned to water in 50 million years.

Valdemar spoke about the smog-like haze that can be seen hanging over this area, indeed over most of the Arctic, when the spring light makes it visible. It first began to be noticed in the 1950s. Global winter and spring wind patterns carry mid-latitude emissions from fossil fuel combustion, smelting and other industrial processes to the Arctic. The cold dense air and the darkness of the Arctic winter allow a build up of these pollutants in the air that is not dispersed until the long days of sunshine arrive. At its worst, the haze covers an area the size of Africa and looks like the pollution that hangs over Los Angeles. The impact of this haze on Arctic eco-systems and the global environment has not been fully researched. It seems likely that the contaminants will end up in the oceans: the Arctic Ocean, the North Atlantic, the Norwegian Sea, the Bering Sea – all of them important fisheries.

Several months later, flying to California from Glasgow, my plane took a northerly route over Iceland and Greenland to avoid strong winds. We flew into the darkness of the northern latitudes, and then curved south into the light again. In a dim twilight I saw the vastness of the icecap stretching into the distance in all directions, broken, hummocked, ridged, crevassed, striated.

Valdemar pointed to a headland a few miles north of the glacier. There his crossing of the icecap had ended. He recounted how, after six weeks on the ice, tears had run down his cheeks at the wonderful smell of vegetation and the feel of rock beneath his feet.

While the others explored the plateau and took photographs, I sat on a flat, scoured rock facing the icecap and composed myself for meditation. The voices of Tom and Marc, the laughter of Cathy and Guylaine drifted into my meditation, blending with the croak of a raven, the rumble of an icefall and the wind rippling across a rock pool to become part of a greater pattern rarely glimpsed. Most of the time we are like a beetle on a Persian carpet. The beetle might be aware of moving from one patch of colour to another as it makes its way across a tiny section of the carpet, but it has no inkling it is crossing a patterned square, one small part of an even grander design; or that the carpet is inside a beautiful room, one of many in a glorious palace.

By previous arrangement, those who had walked to the foot of the glacier, and those who had climbed Nivko had filled their empty thermos flasks with snow. For desert that night we ate a delicious orange and strawberry snow cream, made by pouring concentrated orange juice onto plates piled with snow, making a hollow in the middle and filling it with strawberry jam.

Next morning, watched by several curious caribou, we launched our kayaks, revelling in the luxury of simply slipping them into the water only a few yards away from where the tents had been. Kapisigdlit was the halfway point in our trip. From then on, instead of going mainly eastwards, we would be going mainly westwards, completing the circuit round Qeqertarssuaq Island and finishing where we started, at Nuuk. As we returned up Kapisigdlit Fjord, Valdemar put ashore at the village. He claimed it was to trade some of our coffee for dried whale meat and dried fish. We knew better, we said. He'd arranged an assignation with our temptress of the day before yesterday. Thereafter, till the end of the day, Valdemar was subject to a barrage of corny jokes about looking tired, being more beat than whale meat, less perky than jerky, even weaker than one of Heather's tea bags.

'What was the village like?' I asked Anne, who had chosen to go there yesterday.

She said the people had been very friendly and she'd been invited into several homes for coffee and tinned Danish cookies. Communication was limited but she discovered that the village's population was 113 and that it had its own church, school and grocery shop and was on a hiking circuit from Nuuk, three days being the usual time allowed to get there.

'I think e-mail is very important to the people I met,' Anne said. In a place served by no roads, with no telephone links, and with surface mail arriving by boat only once a month during the summer before the big freeze-over, they depended on it to keep in touch with the outside world.

'I was a bit nervous about going into Kapisigdlit,' Anne confessed. 'I'd heard so many stories of the fierce dogs they keep in places like that which will tear you to pieces given half a chance.'

Luckily, there were no dogs, or she didn't see any.

I quoted the explorer, Knud Rasmusson's comment, 'Give me snow, give me dogs, you can keep the rest,' and how he had written about the thrilling surge of power as 12 or more dogs, harnessed in a fan shape, made the sled skim, hiss and flex over the terrain.

The accounts of those who travelled with dog teams in the old days are full of stories of the savagery of the dogs, fights to the death between rivals, how they might turn on a man if he fell to the ground, or eat a child that came within reach. Joan, who arrived, blades flashing, at this point in our conversation, said that the Greenland sled dogs were not nearly as fierce as they used to be. Partly because dog-sled trips and races play an increasing part in Greenland's growing tourism, the dogs are bred and selected for the non-aggressive qualities. The Greenlanders now mate a bitch with a submissive dog, not the boss dog. Also, when young dogs reach about four months of age, the adult dogs start trying to subordinate them. The pups that do not submit are attacked and often killed – a process of the survival of the submissive.

Dogs were used in the Antarctic as well as in the Arctic. As everyone knows, they were instrumental in helping the Norwegian explorer, Amundsen, to the South Pole in 1911. Since then they have been used by the British Antarctic Survey and other groups in support of scientific work, it being considered that they were safer than vehicles since they were not so heavy and had an instinctive awareness of crevasses. The dogs were also considered to have an important role in keeping up morale in these isolated scientific stations. However, in 1994, the Environmental Protocol banned all dogs from Antarctica. The ban was introduced because of the fear that canine distemper might spread from the dogs to seals, and the possibility that they might break free and disturb or attack native wildlife.

Lunch break was on the widest, sandiest beach we had yet encountered, with the wooden ribs of an old rowing boat poking through the sand and a panoramic view of mountain and fjord. Valdemar offered round the raw dried whale meat. I tried a small piece. It had a very strong, fishy, salty taste, combined with being excessively tough and chewy. A piece smaller than my thumb seemed quite sufficient. Cathy described it as tasting like rubber boots soaked in petrol. I took a photograph of Valdemar chewing happily on a much bigger bit, wondering as I did so if I was guilty of trying to perpetuate some out-dated stereotype of a 'typical Greenlander'. When we were in Nuuk, Valdemar had invited us into his brother's house. I hadn't photographed that, with its modern furniture, packed bookshelves, computer and satellite dish. They say that travellers see the kind of country they want to see. Was this what I was doing?

'What on earth are you agonising about?' Tom demanded. 'He was eating it, wasn't he? And it's more interesting to guys like us than stuff we can see every day at home.'

Maybe I should have been agonising over my own act of eating this endangered species. Somehow, standing on that remote Greenland beach, it didn't feel wrong. Whale meat has been part of the Inuit diet for thousands of

Valdemar eating whale blubber

years and they catch the beasts in ways which are still closer to their traditional hunting methods than to the tactics of mass slaughter adopted by modern whaling ships. At one end of the spectrum of natural resource philosophies are the conservationists who desire to maximise the sustainable yield from certain wildlife populations; at the other end of the spectrum is preservation, the most radical proponents of which seek to banish any human activity which leaves its imprint on lands designated as wilderness. Few organisations concerned with such issues have their headquarters in the Arctic and their staff, boards and members seldom include Arctic residents into whose lives and culture seal and whale hunting is deeply embedded. A Greenlandic hunter is reported as saying in some bewilderment, 'A lady in Paris says we should be vegetarian'. Core values would seem to be in conflict. Native hunters feel they have a right to preserve their culture and traditional way of life. But are they in conflict? Part of the Greenpeace philosophy states, 'As we feel for ourselves, we must feel for all forms of life — the whales, the seals, the forests, the seas'. Native hunters have always identified closely with the animals they hunt, respecting them and showing concern for their souls, and rendering thanks to their prey for the gift of their bodies.

The entries in my diary/journal become rather sparse in the second half of the journey. Tiredness, cold fingers, eagerness to get to the meal, no doubt, all had something to do with it; and not wanting to repeat, yet again, that the icebergs were fantastic, the peaks amazing. My journal certainly didn't bear comparison with those kept by naval officers a century ago, many of which were illustrated to a remarkably high standard. The habit of keeping journals, it seems, was inculcated by making it compulsory for all midshipmen to keep one.

Saturday 23 July

A wonderful and varied day, containing so many of the things I like about kayaking: sheets of sheltered water where we glided through reflected cloud; exposed bits with a lively, exciting motion on the sea; broad skyscapes and landscapes; a brief period of pelting rain puckering the sea all around and making that hissing sound; and good conversations on the way. Saw a large colony of Arctic tern. They are quite small, have black caps, pointed red bills, webbed feet, white bodies and long, white, forked tails. Louis said they are known to be very social birds and always live in large groups. 'One good tern deserves another,' I remarked (rather wittily, I thought).

Later I read up about Arctic tern (*Sterna Paradisaea*) and discovered that they make the longest migration of any bird. At the end of the Arctic summer they fly over 20,000 miles to the Antarctic via Southern Europe, the coast of

One of the larger bergs (courtesy of Chuck Copeland)

West Africa, crossing the Atlantic to South America, arriving in time for the Antarctic summer. They have a life span of about 20 years.

Sunday 24 July

A long paddle, mostly into a head wind. Water clear of ice, except for the occasional floating chunk. Sunglasses on. Anne and Jane, the two housewives and least obviously 'sporty' members of the group, as usual, leave the rest of us behind. 'A lifetime of wringing out the washing and wielding a heavy iron,' is Jane's explanation for this phenomenon. Tent pitched next to a waterfall. Boulders already collected in rings for us! Considering the limited number of possible campsites in these parts it shows how little used this area is that this is the first time there's been a sign of other users. Tom picked mountain/arctic cranberry, which are thick on the ground here and gave me a cupful — red berries, tangy taste. I tried to wash but lost my soap in the torrent. 'If you believe that, you'll believe anything,' was Heather's comment to the others.

Monday 25 July

A long day's paddle, alternating between being warm in the sunshine and frozen by the stiff breeze which kept springing up (we had to plug straight into it). Some biggish bergs, but mostly clear water. We're certainly making up for the views we didn't see during the first week; they change subtly all the time as the mountains present different angles and the entrances to side fjords open up. Finally stopped at 8.00 p.m. as the sun was dipping behind the mountains. Still can't get used to the way the temperature plummets as soon as the sun disappears. Snow and rock of surrounding mountains take on a pinkish glow, but sky remains a pale, greeny-blue. Masses of round, white flowers, known as Labrador Tea (leaves used for this purpose) growing around here. Several big bergs in the bay, two of which turn over in spectacular and impressive fashion. Helped make the supper today. We had mung bean and salami stew, thickened with corn meal, with added chopped onions and garlic. Fresh/whole onions and garlic, rather than the dried variety, are in my opinion worth their weight on any camping trip, and make all the difference to a stew.

I didn't record it in my diary, but I remember, as we huddled together in the tarp late that evening in a variety of awkward sitting or squatting positions, we talked about what it must be like there in winter. It seemed quite cold enough then! Jane said she had read of a seaman, on a polar expedition in the 1820s, who got his hand super-cooled. On putting it into a bucket of cold water, it froze the water. Nuuk itself is one of Greenland's few ice-free ports, but further into the fjord system the fjords freeze over, usually sometime in October. The sea becomes motionless, the water grows viscous, a blue fog of frost smoke detaches itself from the surface, and then the water solidifies, sprouting ice blossoms formed from salt and frozen drops of water.

There seem to be, or there were in the old days, two conflicting versions of the Arctic winter. Some describe it as a time of unending darkness and hardship, a time when the extreme depression known as *perlerorneq* breaks out. The word means 'the weight of life'. The victim tears his clothes, smashes things in the igloo or cabin and runs screaming and half naked into the bitter night. The other version is that winter is a happy time when travelling is at its easiest since you can sledge over the frozen sea. It's a time for visiting, family gatherings and story telling. As for the continual darkness, there are the stars and the moon, the northern lights and reflections off the snow.

Several of the others had seen the northern lights in the Canadian winter. They spoke of fiery waves of light chasing one another across the sky, of interlacing, alternating, pulsating curtains of colour, of sheaves of thousands upon thousands of flashing rays.

'They're the souls of all our stillborn children,' Valdemar said.

'And which do you prefer, Valdemar? Summer or winter?'

'The winter: the winter is something special.'

Anders, a Norwegian writer, had already said something similar to me when I told him I was going to Tromsö in Arctic Norway and was looking forward to experiencing the midnight sun. Incidentally, his name was not Anders, but he asked me to call him that because, he said, my attempts to pronounce his real name were too painful to him. He was of the opinion that the streets tunnelling through 20 feet of snow, the stillness and the northern lights were even more impressive than the perpetual daylight.

We talked about the careful preparations for Arctic over wintering made by the masters of the old sailing ships. After selecting a sheltered bay, the ship's upper works were dismantled, leaving only the lower masts standing. If this wasn't done, the accumulated weight of ice and rime could dismast or capsize the ship. The upper decks were packed with a foot or more of snow for insulation and this was then sanded. The upper decks were then roofed and sided with canvas so that the crew could exercise in shelter. Fire holes were sawn in the ice that had formed round the ship and kept open all winter in case water was needed to extinguish a fire.

Tuesday 26 July

Mist soon lifted. Glorious paddle down the fjord called Umanap Suvdlua, in flat calm, with many iceberg reflections in aquamarine, beryl and other shades of green; clouds projecting out of high valleys; snow slopes glistening; short day. Our lunch place also our camp place. Washed in stream — water very

The crews of HM Ships Hecla *and* Griper *cutting into winter harbour,*
September 26th 1819 (from Parry's Journal of a Voyage *by Alexander Fisher, 1820)*

HM Ships Hecla *and* Griper *in winter harbour*
(from Parry's Journal of a Voyage *by Alexander Fisher, 1820)*

cold, but invigorating. This is almost like a meadow (almost, I said), with Arctic blueberry, harebell, fleabane (like a daisy), crowberry, chamomile, dandelion and broad-leaved willow herb (the national flower of Greenland) Watched a balletic berg dance by in the strong current of the narrows between us and a little island, gracefully twisting and turning, showing all its varieties of form. Lay in the sun.

'Lay in the sun' doesn't seem like anything very memorable, but it was luxury indeed. I had time for reflection, time to listen to the sounds of nature, watch the clouds, feel the earth turning and appreciate the moment. Appreciate the moment was all I could do. Nobody observes the land more keenly than a hungry hunter; nobody understands a corner of the earth better than someone who has experienced it in every season and every mood, who has seen it in a thousand different lights, known its sounds, felt its textures after the first frost, or smelt its fragrance after rain. That kind of intimacy would never be mine. With sadness I acknowledged that I'd never know Greenland in the way that the Inuit hunters knew their land. My acquaintance with this ancient land of rock and ice could never be anything but a fleeting and superficial one, even though I felt in tune with its austere magnificence.

The following day we enjoyed a similar weather pattern with low strips of cloud in the morning cutting the mountains in two, making the peaks seem remote and disembodied. Then, in the early afternoon, the cloud dissolved into brilliant blue sky. We started paddling at noon and finished at 8.30 pm, the mountains maintaining their magnificence throughout the day: domes, towers, sheer walls of smooth rock rising out of the water, dazzling snow, until I was almost punch-drunk with scenery. Awestruck, we passed under one of the highest, sheerest cliffs I've ever paddled beneath; acres of smooth vertical yellow-brown rock reduced us to silence.

Out of a clear blue sky, a hailstorm hit us. Hailstones thudded into canvas, or rattled and bounced on fibreglass, making moon-craters in the smooth sea, stinging faces, turning decks and water and raised hoods white. Then, as suddenly as it came, it was over and the sky was blue again. Soon after this we encountered a motor cabin cruiser. A man and a woman appeared on deck and shouted greetings and waved a coffee pot at us. We came alongside while mugs of very welcome, strong, hot coffee were handed down, to be shared one between two since there weren't enough mugs to go round. The man, whose name was Kristian Olsen, spoke excellent English. He said he and his wife were on holiday from Denmark and were out for a day's fishing. He showed us a bucketful of Norway haddock he'd caught that morning. By high-powered boat, he said, Nuuk was only about three hours away. I don't think any of us were quite ready to end our brief but passionate affair with the wilderness. Kristian was

The home run — spectacular mountains

interested in our kayaks. Most summers, he said, they went kayak camping in the Swedish Archipelago.

Unlike me, he had been to the Kayak Museum in Nuuk. He had also been to the Fram Museum in Oslo, Norway, and seen the bamboo and canvas kayak which the Norwegian polar explorer, Fridtjof Nansen had used to return from his attempt to reach the North Pole in 1895. About seven years before that, while on the east coast of Greenland, making slow and laborious progress through ice floes in a heavy rowing boat, Nansen had encountered two Eskimos in kayaks who negotiated the tricky waters with much greater speed and ease than he and his crew. He had been so impressed that he decided to copy their craft and make use of it in future expeditions. We discussed how, in Britain at least, early kayaks were like rowing boats pointed at both ends. It took a while before they began to look like Inuit kayaks, or for there to be any appreciation that perhaps the Inuit knew what they were doing. The British Arctic explorer, Gino Watkins, was the first to bring the Eskimo kayak to the attention of the British public when he returned from Greenland in the early 1930s with a kayak the local hunters had made for him, and gave demonstrations of kayak rolling. There are many different designs of Inuit kayak, each adapted to the conditions of the area, but Gino's East Greenland design was the one that became best know in Britain. Not until the late 1960s, however, were Greenland designs consciously copied by British kayak builders, albeit in fibreglass, and sold commercially.

It was time to move on. We thanked Kristian and his wife for the coffee and continued on our way. Before long, though, the sight of those fish Kristian had caught became too much for Marc and Joan. We stopped in the lee of another towering rock wall on the north side of the fjord. Here Marc and Joan got out their rods and lures. Between them they caught half a dozen Norway haddock in as many minutes. The water was so clear we could see shoals of fish and huge boulders 30 feet down.

About four miles further on, still dominated by huge cliffs, reminders of our own puny, ephemeral existence, we hauled out for a quick brew-up on an island of polished, grained rock, no more than 800 metres in length and 200 metres wide. I love islands you can walk right round in a short space of time, that you can stand in the middle of and see the whole of them and to which the Crusoe inside you can lay claim. It is part of the lure of islands of this size, I think, that they fit inside your heart.

In talking about his crossing of the icecap, Valdemar had said he'd sometimes longed for a bit of colour to relieve the whiteness. On Greenland's coastline, in summer, there is certainly no lack of colour: the sea flashing bottle green, shores ablaze with purple saxifrage, cranberry, blue harebells and bright green moss, and the icebergs glowing like stained-glass windows.

Fishing for our supper

That evening we feasted on wonderfully fresh fish, seasoned with a stupendous view across the fjord, white bergs dotting the bright blue water, snowfields accentuating the curves and edges of the mountains over which rode a big yellow half moon. We talked about bears, not polar bears this time, but the grizzly and brown bears that inhabit the wilderness areas of the Canadian Pacific coast and the Alaska coast. My Canadian companions swapped stories of the dangers of having your food supplies anywhere near your tent. The bears have a well-developed sense of smell and are quite likely to come into a tent looking for the food. The standard advice for wilderness campers in these areas is to cook all food well away from the tent and then to change out of the clothes you wore while cooking before retiring for the night — after having hung your food from a branch at least 12 feet off the ground. And there was no shortage of horror stories about tourists, brought up on TV cartoons about Yogi Bear and Pooh Bear, who really believe that bears are cuddly, cute, friendly creatures. One story was about a man whom a Park Ranger found trying to shove a brown bear into the front seat of his car, next to his wife, because he thought it would be amusing to snap them sitting together. Another, which had tragic consequences, involved a couple that wanted a holiday photograph of a bear holding their baby.

At two in the morning, when the meal was over and people had started to drift back to their tents, I wandered up the hillside in the twilight and was surprised to see Cathy and Joan higher up with the same idea. As I sat there I relived a winter ascent of Ben Ime by moonlight, where acres of snow sparkled in a way never seen by day. I thought about a midnight paddle to celebrate the longest day of the year, accompanied by a long, lingering sunset over Mull which passed through a thousand different shades of red and purple. And I recalled a night on Loch Lomond, gliding down a silvery path laid by the moon when three red deer swam across my bows – an almost mystical experience. Truly wild, free animals have an aura of otherness and of connection to a primal world now lost to us. And yet their wildness has a magnetic quality. It calls to something deep inside us.

Thursday 28 July

A windy, choppy second half to the day as we approached the mouth of the fjord system and open water. More cliffs plunging into the sea. Campsite within two or three hours of Nuuk, should be there tomorrow. Marc has worked out that, allowing for detours, criss-crossing the fjords to reach the best (sometimes the only) campsites, and other little side-trips, we have probably paddled about 150 nautical miles. Compared to other longer and more dangerous Greenland expeditions one reads about, this has been a fairly humble and 'user friendly' trip. For all that, it has been an unforgettable and deeply felt experience. Saw the sun sink below the sea for the first time, as up till now the mountains enclosing the fjords have hidden this sight from us. Did meditation outside the tent, facing the afterglow of the sun.

> *There is joy*
> *In feeling the warmth*
> *Come to the great world*
> *And seeing the sun*
> *Follow its old footprints*
> *In the summer night.*   (From a traditional Inuit poem)

Floating in a small rock pool in the middle of a patch of bright green moss was an empty beer bottle, the first signs of the proximity of 'civilisation'. My initial reaction was to regard the bottle as litter and pollution. Then it struck me that a Martian looking at it might think it was beautiful. It was beautiful: the way the light refracted as it passed through it, the patterns it sent dancing over the water, the way its glassiness and greenness echoed the icebergs in the bay. Andy Warhol, of course, has said all this to us in his paintings of squashed coke and soup cans. I have a photograph of what people take to be a Himalayan range of mountains. They exclaim over the beauty of the gleaming knife-edge ridges, the fluted flanks of ice, the sparkling peaks. In fact, it's a photograph of a piece of plastic sheeting that was lying on the beach near my house. And I remember sitting in a snow hole, high up on a Scottish mountain, watching a distant glow in the sky. When I thought it was the herald of dawn I saw it as beautiful, but when I realised it was the lights of Glasgow its attraction faded.

Earlier on the trip I had been thinking about how the British painters of a century ago saw the wilderness as hostile. They were reflecting the general perception and taste of those times. Travellers thought of mountainous regions as dangerous, horrible and uninviting. Only later were they transformed in the European imagination into exciting, uplifting, beautiful places. A similar transformation occurred in how people saw the Arctic. There's a kind of latent aggression in Western society that leads to a confrontational approach to things. In Parliament we have a party of opposition whose function is to oppose, no matter what. Our legal system is adversarial with two sides battling it out, often with truth and justice as the victims. Western surgery flourishes on the principal of cutting out the offending part, rather than treating the whole person or looking for cures that are not based on an arsenal of knives, laser guns and other weaponry. As far as the Arctic is concerned it was the explorer Vilhjalmur

Stefansson, born in Canada of Icelandic parents, who probably did more than any other person to change this attitude. Although Charles Frances Hall had preceded him in using Inuit knowledge and techniques, Stefansson's book *The Friendly Arctic* (1921) was the first of its kind, expounding a philosophy of living in harmony with the landscape rather than fighting it. My relationship with the sea has been rather similar. At first I went out in my kayak to do battle with the waves. Only when I took to meditation did I begin to feel that the ocean was part of me and I was part of it. I became more relaxed, more in harmony with the rhythms of the sea and my kayaking improved.

Stefansson, by the way, couldn't have found the Arctic all that friendly because his 'Arctic Manual' contains instructions on how to eat your kayak if you're really starving and thereby avoid cannibalism. Rawhide, which by definition hasn't been tanned, is quite nutritious. His manual discusses whether it's better to eat your boat, your boots or your clothing first. 'Wearing a garment is a cheaper and easier way of securing body warmth than eating it,' he solemnly advises.

'I wonder what's for breakfast tomorrow,' Louis muttered sleepily as I crawled back into the tent.

'It might just be your welly boots.... and they'd taste like whale meat soaked in petrol, I shouldn't wonder.'

'As long as it is petrol, Robin, and not something else!'

The next day, Nuuk came into sight, the smudges of colour gradually separating out into individual houses. And then, with mixed feelings, we were landing in the bay from which we'd set out. I felt sad because it was ending, relieved that the discomforts and physical toil were over, elated at having achieved what I'd set out to do. Nuuk, which had struck me as a fairly sparse, basic sort of place all those days ago, now seemed the height of luxury and civilisation. Hot showers and drying rooms and proper beds!

That evening, washed and shaved and sweet-smelling, hardly recognizing each other or ourselves in our clean city clothes, we gathered in a hotel for a meal that was both a celebration and a farewell. There, at the bar, was our friend we'd met out on the fjord, Kristian Olsen.

He was, I discovered, a professor of Arctic Literature at a Danish university. He explained to me that, although the Arctic region is divided between eight different countries – USA, Canada, Russia, Iceland, Norway, Sweden, Finland – the minority native populations of these countries have a great deal in common and a growing unity. The map of the world found in most atlases uses the Mercator's projection, which shows the Arctic regions stretching from one side of the double page to the other. 'It still influences how people think of the Arctic and see it in their minds,' he said. In reality, of course, or when looked at on a globe, the Arctic countries circle the Polar Sea and are comparatively close to each other, with a common climate and very similar flora and fauna. The Inuit of Alaska, Canada and Greenland all speak much the same language and possess a common culture, and the Sami (Lapps) of Norway, Sweden, Finland and Russia similarly share a language and culture that is basically the same. The Inuit Circumpolar Conference assists the Inuit people, irrespective of which country governs them, with land claims and efforts towards self-determination; and there are moves in that direction to recognise the rights of the Sami people despite the international borders that try to divide them. Kristian talked about the problems of being a writer in languages and dialects that have such a small readership. Publications were heavily dependent on government subsidies. It was sometimes difficult, he said, to persuade the givers of grants to realize that the artistic output of hunter-gatherer people did not divide neatly into our accepted categories of literature, music, drama and so forth, but was much more multi-skilled. Inuit poetry could not be separated from drumming and ritual dance, and the *Sami Yoik* was not quite poetry, nor quite song, but something unique. The arts of minority people, he thought, were vital if these groups were to retain their identity and resist powerful influences from outside. The languages of hunters, Kristian said, had fine nuances of description and were well adapted to writing about the landscape, nature and the wilderness. They were the languages of people who listened to the heart of the earth.

Our departure from Nuuk was as laid back as our entry. So much so that Louis and I wandered onto the runway, climbed a ladder onto the nearest plane and settled in before we found out it was the wrong plane. We scrambled off and enquired of the next one along if it was, by any chance, going to Iqaluit.

'*Imaaqa*, maybe,' came the reply from the hostess in the doorway.

As we headed across Davis Strait, back to Iqaluit on Baffin Island there was no babble of conversation such as there'd been on the outward journey. The writer, Peter Matthiessen, describing a descent from the Himalayas, likened it to rejoining the world after a religious retreat. 'It is crucial to emerge gradually from such a chrysalis, drying new wings in the sun's quiet, like a butterfly, to avoid a sudden tearing of the spirit.'

We were flying on much the same bearing the Vikings had followed when, nine centuries earlier, they'd sailed from west Greenland and made landfall on Baffin Island. Historians still argue about what route they took from there. The most commonly held opinion is that they voyaged south, reaching Labrador and Newfoundland. There is a hypothesis, however, that they sailed north, and that the expedition described in the sagas wintered at Coronation Gulf on Canada's northern coast. Stefansson provided corroborating evidence for this when he reported seeing blonde Eskimos in the area. Wherever it was they went, the accounts agree that they met Indians. Friendly at first and willing to trade, the Indians turned hostile when a bull, brought by the Vikings in one of their open boats, charged bellowing out of the woods. Taking this to be some kind of evil spirit in the service of the strangers, the Indians withdrew, returning later to attack the Viking encampment. Not wishing to spend the winter under siege, the Vikings sailed away never to return. But for that bull the history of Canada might have been quite different.

The last views of Greenland vanished behind white vapour. On leaving Alaska, John Muir wrote: 'Your heart will cry every day for the north like a lost child and in your sleep the snow banners of the white peaks will beckon to you'. Yes, already Greenland was calling me back. In that billion-year-old landscape the roots of things, both physical and human, had seemed less hidden. For a while, like the Inuit, I had felt close to nature. I'd experienced hardship and simplicity and the contentment of doing one thing at a time. There, where the earth spins at its slowest, I'd had time to return into myself. Greenland, a Zen garden in the Arctic, a place for meditation, a place for discovering one's own inner landscape, a place for journeying in the imagination. Perhaps it was enough simply to have been there, to respond to the light, the icebergs, the scale of things, the timelessness. The explorer Elisha Kent Kane recorded the words of a companion overawed by the beauty of West Greenland: 'Maybe we have lived only to be here now'. Or, as Gerard Manley Hopkins expressed it, 'These things, these things were here and but the beholder wanting'.

The airhostess came down the aisle offering newspapers. The modern world and all its problems was with us once more.

'Everything's suddenly speeding up!' Carol exclaimed, echoing my thoughts. 'It's all coming to an end so fast!'

'But the memories will last,' Tom reassured her.

Perhaps they will, but like the icebergs, I think they'll gradually change shape and melt and become part of the ocean of my being. In fact, the process has already begun.

There's an old Inuit saying that 'all songs are born in man out in the great wilderness'.

In Greenland I had listened to the heart of the earth and now it is like a song inside me, sometimes faint, but always there.